Making the Peace

"*Making the Peace* is an innovative resource, a breakthrough in the journey to prevent violence. It offers a step-by-step process of looking at many causes of violence among youth. The sessions are relatively easy to follow and they create a comfortable and non-threatening arena where youth can voice their fears, frustrations and solutions about violence. Particularly impressive, the authors broaden the issue of violence by presenting underlying causes such as gender roles, societal expectations, economic class, power, race and the self-realization of violence. The action component of the manual also presents the unique term of 'ally' that captures the essence of how people can develop to be proponents for peace. *Making the Peace* is a valuable resource for youth workers, teachers, educators and concerned parents." — **Ariel D. San Pedro, Director of Ethnic Youth Ministry, Diocese of Oakland**

"Included in the curriculum are all the materials a teacher needs to address issues that are difficult to discuss openly, issues that become even more difficult when they're *not* discussed openly. Teachers are given very practical guidance through a classroom discussion process that would fit in almost any subject area. From describing how the desks should be arranged in the room to facilitate a free-flowing discussion, to helping teachers anticipate potential rough spots, Creighton and Kivel seem to have given a great deal of thought to what works in a classroom and what is helpful for the teacher. As a teacher and as a teacher trainer, I appreciate the fact that Mr. Creighton and Mr. Kivel acknowledge the challenges that teachers face daily." — **Helen Duffy, Pinole Valley High School teacher and Supervisor of Teacher Education, U.C. Berkeley**

"Working from the core of the issues, *Making the Peace* identifies clear strategies, pinpoints the skills needed to achieve them, and provides the information necessary to prepare for each session. From the genesis of violence, both personal and societal, this comprehensive curriculum provides guidance in becoming allies, healing the heart, conflict resolution and mediation, and community action. *Making the Peace* should be a required course of learning and action for everyone from the President to members of Congress, from athletes and entertainers to inner city youths and young people in rural communities." — **Daphne Muse, author of** *Prejudice: Stories about Hate, Ignorance, Revelation and Transformation*

About the Oakland Men's Project

The Oakland Men's Project is a multiracial, community-based violence prevention program, operating since 1979, dedicated to eliminating men's violence and promoting cross-gender and cross-racial alliances. Through education with youth and adults and through community organizing, OMP reaches high school and junior high adolescents and teachers, parents, social service professionals, and religious, civic, governmental, and correctional organizations throughout the state of California and across the country. OMP may be reached at:

Oakland Men's Project
1203 Preservation Park Way, Suite 200
Oakland CA 94612
Tel. (510) 835-2433
Fax: (510) 835-2466

About the cover design

When I was given the job of designing an identity for the Making the Peace project, I sat and thought of possible imagery to represent violence prevention. Many negative images came to my mind—guns, drugs, peer pressure, hate—all things that today's young people have to deal with in their lives. However, none of these carried the message that I wanted to send: hope. So I sat and thought some more, and came up with the image of a patchwork quilt, a traditional American art. But I wanted to create a patchwork that was really American, for today. I researched different traditional designs and folk art, and a design gradually evolved that was made up of ethnic patterns and symbols that represent the diversity that makes up America. While each pattern is exciting and unique on its own, together they make something beautiful that is even stronger. And yet you can see how close some of these original folk designs are to each other. So my design celebrates diversity, and it celebrates unity, because I believe it is the combination of these two things that make a country truly great.

—Jil Weil, Oakland, California

A 15-Session Violence Prevention Curriculum for Young People

Paul Kivel and Allan Creighton
with the Oakland Men's Project

With contributions from Lakota Harden and Heru-Nefera Amen

Hunter House
PUBLISHERS

Library of Congress Cataloging-in-Publication Data

Kivel, Paul.
Making the Peace: a 15-session curriculum for young people / Paul Kivel and Allan Creighton with the Oakland Men's Project.—1st ed.
p. cm. — (Making the peace)
Includes bibliographical references.
ISBN 0-89793-205-6 (pbk.)
1. Violence—Prevention—Study and teaching (Secondary)—United States.
2. School violence—Prevention—Study and teaching (Secondary)—United States. 3. Conflict management—Study and teaching (Secondary)—United States. 4. Peace—Study and teaching (Secondary)—United States.
I. Creighton, Allan. II. Oakland Men's Project. III. Title. IV. Series.

HN90.V5K54 1996	373.17'82—dc20	96-34103	CIP

Ordering

Hunter House books are available for textbook/course adoptions and are sold at bulk discounts to qualifying community, healthcare and government organizations for internal use, resale, special promotions, or fundraising. For details please contact

Special Sales Department
Hunter House Inc., PO Box 2914, Alameda CA 94501-0914
Tel. (510) 865-5282 Fax (510) 865-4295
e-mail: marketing@hunterhouse.com

Individuals can order our books from most bookstores or by calling toll-free:

1-800-266-5592

Cover Design and Logo: Jil Weil, Oakland
Book design: Janet Wood
Project Editors: Lisa E. Lee, Jane E. Moore
Development/Copyediting: Mali Apple
Marketing: Corrine M. Sahli
Customer Support: Sharon R.A. Olson, Edgar M. Estavilla, Jr., A & A Quality Shipping
Publisher: Kiran S. Rana

Logo 3-D fimo illustration: Christine Benjamin
Production: Paul J. Frindt, Kiran S. Rana
Editorial Assistance: Tami Wisniewski
Proofreaders: Lee Rappold, Kim A. Wallace
Promotion & Publicity: Kim A. Wallace

Printed and bound by Data Reproductions Corporation, Rochester Hills, MI
Manufactured in the United States of America

9 8 7 6 5   First edition

List of Contents

List of Handouts

List of On Your Own Exercises

Exercise Permissions and Credits

(These credits are an extension of the copyright page)
Heart Exercise (pp. 44–46, 48) used with permission from Lakota Harden © 1997 Lakota Harden.
Sexual harassment scenario (pp. 125–126) excerpted from *Sexual Harassment and Teens: A Program
for Positive Change* by Susan Strauss with Pamela Espeland, ©1992. Used with permission from
Free Spirit Publishing Inc., Minneapolis, MN (800) 735-7323, all rights reserved. Ally Pledge
(pp. 66, 161) adapted from *Young Men's Work: Building Skills to Stop Violence* by Allan Creighton
and Paul Kivel, ©1994, the Oakland Men's Project. Used with permission from Hazelden
Publishing, Center City, MN (800) 328-9000. Various exercises (Agreements: pp. 46–47, 49; Power
Chart: pp. 52–58; Adultism Visualization: pp. 68–69; Youth Stand-Up: pp. 69–71; White Stand-Up:
pp. 86–90; People of Color Stand-Up, pp. 90–93; People of Color Speak-Out: p. 93–94;
Father-Son Role Play: p. 106–107; Act-Like-a-Man Box: pp. 107–109, 114; Act-Like-a-Lady Box:
pp. 110–112, 116; Men's Step-Out: p. 122–123; Women's Step-Out: p. 123–124) adapted from
Helping Teens Stop Violence: A Practical Guide for Counselors, Educators and Parents by Allan Creighton
with Paul Kivel, ©1992, the Oakland Men's Project. Used with permission from Hunter House
Inc., Alameda, CA (800) 266-5592.

Acknowledgments

Our deepest thanks to —

Isoke Femi, Nell Myhand, and Hugh Vasquez of TODOS Institute for guidance, wisdom, and partnership;

Ricky Sherover-Marcuse and Harrison Simms for vision;

Teresa Brown, Lakota Harden, Victor Lewis, Marcelle Moran, and Jackie Schonerd for their original contributions to the work;

Ralph Cantor for years of unfailing support of OMP and testing of materials with young people;

Julie Nesnansky for keeping us clear on the needs of working teachers;

Lisa Lee, Mali Apple, and Kiran Rana of Hunter House for their editorial rigor and guidance;

Young people and teachers across the state of California whose lives, making the peace day-to-day, continue to inspire us.

The contributions of Heru-Nefera Amen, Program Director for the Oakland Men's Project, are too numerous to detail. His political and spiritual vision, his commitment to racial and gender justice, and his many years of profound work with young people and adults in workshops, classes and trainings in making the peace have informed every page of this manual. With Lakota Harden and others mentioned above he has helped to create orally the model which is put into writing here.

Making the Peace

Before You Begin

The Making the Peace curriculum is a complete program offering you everything you need to address violence prevention in your classroom, after-school or residential program, or juvenile justice setting. You will find that young people are often eager and anxious to talk about these issues and to develop alternatives to violence. This self-guiding curriculum provides them an opportunity to do just that—with your support. Here are some brief suggestions for beginning.

Start by reading the Introduction to prepare for running the sessions and working with young people. The topics discussed will help you assess your resources and environment and think strategically about where you need to start. Do you have more young women than young men in your class? Are you in a rural area? An inner city? Is your class predominantly white? Predominantly students of color?

Next, the assessment questionnaire on pages 29–31 will help you evaluate your school setting and social environment so you can adapt your work accordingly.

Last, read through the fifteen sessions. They contain detailed information about how to lead the exercises and guide the discussions. The "What if . . . " section that follows many sessions offers suggestions for how to deal with typical responses from young people. The suggestions will help you prepare for particular situations you might encounter such as recent violent incidents in the school, guns on campus, or reporting situations in which students are experiencing physical or sexual violence.

The curriculum, although filled with step-by-step instructions about how to proceed, is meant to be adapted to your particular needs. You could use it every day for fifteen days, or once a week for fifteen weeks. Parts of the curriculum can be incorporated into social living, health, social studies, or current issues courses. If you work with youth more intensively, the sessions can be combined in two-, three-, or six-hour workshops around specific themes. Other ideas for using this curriculum will come to you as you read through the Introduction.

In whatever form you use *Making the Peace,* spend more time on some sections and less on others as you let students pursue areas they are excited about or that speak to their needs and concerns. The issues are too important to students' lives—and to their ability to accomplish academic work—for them to be presented quickly or inflexibly. Young people need to be actively engaged in defining, discussing, and strategizing about these issues so that they can truly take leadership in making the peace in their lives. Their ownership of the curriculum is the gauge of your success.

The curriculum begins with five sessions that introduce basic concepts and provide a framework of safety and respect for the class to operate within. Session 1 introduces concepts of violence and safety and helps students think about how violence affects their lives. Session 2 defines violence and creates group agreements to build a climate of safety for subsequent sessions. Session 3 looks at the causes of violence in social, political, and economic inequality and how these create a cycle of violence. Session 4 introduces the core concept of being an ally—how we can take an active role in making the peace and stopping self-destructive violence, interpersonal violence, and violence caused by social injustice. Session 5 focuses on how violence is learned and what kinds of violence happen to young people.

These five sessions set the groundwork for the next six sessions, which look at the particular forms that violence takes. Sessions 6 and 7 look at alternatives to intra- and interracial violence and anti-Semitism. Session 8 helps young people understand how violence can be rooted in economic issues. Sessions 9 and 10 look at gender relationships and present tools for preventing physical and sexual violence toward women. Session 11 examines strategies for reducing violence associated with guns and other weapons.

The last four sessions focus on healing from past experiences of violence, on individual and group action, and on youth leadership in making the peace at different levels, including the personal (Session 12), interpersonal (Sessions 13 and 14), and social (Session 15).

These sessions set the stage for ongoing activities that young people define and direct. The handouts in Session 15 describe different directions young people may choose to follow up on as active allies to themselves and to each other.

Once you have read and are familiar with the sessions, review and make copies of the handouts and On Your Own sheets, put up the posters (if you have purchased them), and talk with other staff about your goals for the curriculum. Reread the "Being an Ally to Young People" section in the introduction (see pages 13–16), especially the section on getting support.

Welcome to this challenging and rewarding work! By leading your students through this curriculum, you too are making the peace.

Introduction

"Peace is not the absence of conflict, but the presence of justice."
— Martin Luther King Jr.

Violence is a powerful—and troubling—factor in American life. We may all agree that some things people do to one another, like beating and homicide, are violent. We may strongly disagree about whether other things, like spanking children to discipline them, are forms of violence. For most of us, however, the first response to the issue of violence is fear.

Headlines emphasize the bloody, brutal, random, and senseless aspects of violence. We are inundated with information and advice about who is vulnerable, who does the hurting, how to stay safe, and who is to blame. Young people are in the headlines on both sides: as abducted children and victims of drive-by shootings, and as gun-wielding gang members. We have learned to fear for our children *and* to be afraid of them.

Fear distorts our sense of the world and incapacitates us. To begin to prevent violence, we must move beyond fear and develop an understanding of what violence actually is.

The Roots of Violence

One thing we do know is that most violence occurs among people who know each other. Homicide, sexual assault, family violence, fights between students—over 90 percent of all violence in this country is committed not by strangers, but by friends, dates, family members, coworkers, or classmates. Furthermore, 95 percent of all physical and sexual violence is committed by men. In other words, most interpersonal acts of violence involve men hurting women, other men, or children whom they know.

These facts have two implications. First, violence happens when the social bonds of a community break down and violence between people who know each other is tolerated, expected, condoned, or praised. Rebuilding those community bonds is a requisite for peace.

Second, we must look to the gender-role training that teaches young men to use violence to establish who they are and to get their needs met. Young women can also be violent, but they are not systematically conditioned to use violence to meet their needs. When young women are violent, they are acting out male-constructed models of power and aggression. Reducing the effects of gender-role training, or eliminating this training altogether, is the second essential step toward making the peace.

Helping Young People Make Peace

The subject of this curriculum is violence among and against young people: what it is, where it comes from, and how to stop it. The goal is to help young people understand and heal from violence, to come together as a community to make the peace. In the words of Martin Luther King Jr., "Violence is anything that denies human integrity, and leads to hopelessness and helplessness." The Making the Peace curriculum is built on the idea that violence is whatever hinders, limits, or damages us as human beings, including not only direct hurt but the long-term internalized effects of that hurt.

High-profile violent acts are usually rooted in *structural violence*—the deep, underlying social and economic inequalities that are drawn across lines of race, gender, age, and sexual orientation in our society. Visible acts in which one person hurts another are one place where structural violence shows up. Interpersonal violence of any kind cannot be prevented unless we address these structural roots.

When two young Latino men get into a fight with each other, it is not just a matter of two guys losing control or fighting for their self-respect. Lack of job opportunities, inadequate schools, the internalization of racial stereotypes, and male gender-role training in competition and violence all contribute to setting these two people up to fight, and perhaps kill, each other. More than anger-management skills are needed to incorporate them into a community of peers committed to working cooperatively with each other to make the peace.

Young people—in particular, young men—are caught in the middle of the dynamics of structural violence. They are vulnerable to physical, sexual, and emotional violence from adults at the same time they are being trained to assume adult roles that entail the control and abuse of others.

By ourselves, we can neither stop the violence nor protect young people from it. But, working together with young people, we can take action that will reduce the social inequality at the roots of violence and reclaim and restore the human integrity that violence denies.

As long as there are people, there will be conflict among them. Interpersonal conflict is a healthy, normal part of any community. Beyond making the peace, this curriculum can help young people and adults learn techniques for resolving interpersonal conflict, welcome their differences, and begin the long process of achieving justice.

The Components of the Making the Peace Curriculum

The Oakland Men's Project has conducted classes, workshops, and trainings with young people, parents, and professionals since 1979 on preventing violence and fostering social justice. The Making the Peace curriculum represents our best thinking to date about how to facilitate this work with young people.

The Making the Peace curriculum is designed to help you assist and guide the youth you work with, teach, or live with to come together as a community to end violence. It includes the following components:

Making the Peace Curriculum Guide

This curriculum or facilitator's guide contains all the information you need to facilitate fifteen classroom sessions—the core curriculum—and to use the student handouts and the posters. It presents step-by-step instructions for the sessions, anticipates difficult issues you may face, and offers ideas for follow-up both within the class and within your school or youth program.

The student handouts and On Your Own sheets are laid out in the text for easy reproduction. Once you have distributed them, do not collect them, read them, or mark them. Assure students that no one else will see their handouts. They are a vital part of each session *for the students*. They are also a written record that students can keep of the work they have done, the ideas they have been introduced to, and the feelings and thoughts they have about the material.

If possible, provide or ask students to obtain inexpensive folders in which to keep all of the handouts and assignments. Students will often want to refer to their previous work in class, so remind them to bring their folders to every session.

The handouts contain information, exercises, and group activities that extend the learning process more deeply into students' lives as well as out into the community. Give students time to read the handouts in class and to jot down comments or responses. The On Your Own assignments are to help students reflect on the session's content after class or to prepare them for upcoming material. You will find it useful to begin most sessions with time for comments on the On Your Own assignments and any other reflections students have on previous material.

You know your students, their abilities, their interests, and their level of motivation. You may not be able to expect them to complete the On Your Own sheets. However, these assignments contain basic information and thought-provoking questions that the students, their friends, and families will benefit from considering or discussing. Encourage them to talk about the issues that are raised with friends and family members outside of class if they feel comfortable in doing so.

Making the Peace Posters

The Making the Peace posters are designed to be used in your classroom and throughout the school to publicize the program, to reinforce the basic themes, and to rally students' energy and excitement. They will contribute to an atmosphere within the class or school that emphasizes a community based on caring intervention and leadership on the part of young people. The posters will inspire hope, challenge cynicism, and confront prejudices and misinformation. They can also be used to encourage youth to develop their own posters, symbols, and other visual images to express what they are learning.

Days of Respect Organizer's Manual

Days of Respect is a schoolwide organizing program designed to help change the school environment into one in which students are active and empowered to increase respect and decrease violence. The Days of Respect program can be used as a follow-up to the fifteen-session core curriculum, as a precursor to this or other violence-prevention programs, or as an independent program.

The Days of Respect program relies on training a group of students, parents, and teachers to lead an entire student body through a series of exercises, speak-outs, and discussions. The program helps establish the need for and provide the tools to achieve a respectful school environment in which students, teachers, staff, and parents are working together to make the peace.

The *Days of Respect* organizer's manual provides everything you need to run an exciting and inspiring Days of Respect program at your school. It includes outlines, timelines, handouts, agendas, training exercises, a guide for media outreach, and step-by-step guidelines for implementing the program.

Working with Youth to Make the Peace

As an adult who cares about and works with youth, you play a crucial role in their lives. When you begin to explore the subject of violence with them, you start a process that will involve you in two companion challenges.

First, young people have *all* been hurt by violence—from disrespect and belittlement to beatings and sexual abuse—and almost always at the hands of adults. Concerning sexual abuse alone, one out of four girls and one out of six boys will be sexually assaulted before the age of eighteen.[*] While violence prevention does not rest upon the disclosure of such experiences, you can assume that if you make it safe for young people to talk about violence, you will hear about how they have been hurt. You may be surprised and upset at the amount and

---

[*] Russell, Diana E. H. "The Incidence and Prevalence of Intrafamilial and Extrafamilial Sexual Abuse of Female Children." In *Handbook of Sexual Abuse of Children,* edited by Lenore E. A. Walker. New York: Springer Publishing, 1988.

degree of violence they have already experienced. You may be discouraged to find that you are seen as part of the problem; because of their experiences, many young people are highly suspicious of adults. Some see you as the enemy. And many will expect, with some justification, that adults will lecture them about violence in much the same way they lecture about drug abuse and sex—telling them that their behavior is the problem and that all they need do is behave better. Young people may also have had adults tell them one thing and then practice another, making them mistrustful of the motives of adults. Overcoming all the obstacles brought on by students' prior experiences may be one of the greatest—and most rewarding—challenges of teaching this curriculum.

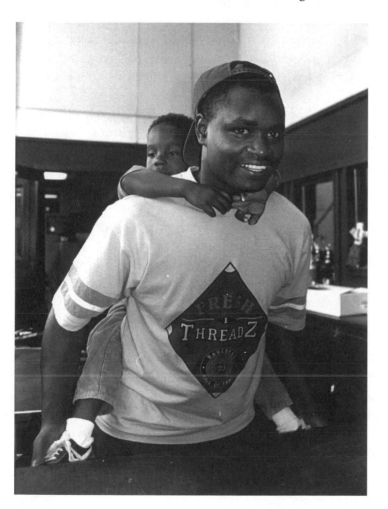

Second, we also have our *own* histories of violence and violation. Most of us are still affected by significant, painful experiences of our own childhood and youth. Listening attentively to young people discuss these issues can be difficult; their experiences can remind us of our own unresolved memories. Moreover, in our roles as adults, we are responsible not only for our own lives but for the lives of young people as well—and as parents and teachers, we are overworked and often lack the necessary time, patience, or attention to help young people cope with so much.

In our favor in dealing with these challenges is that we are *adults* taking a stand with young people against violence. We have information, useful experience, and resources to offer, and we want to create a world free from violence. Also, young people can be inspiring examples for each other and for us, and they help share the responsibilities for making the world safe—and that will pay us back many times over for our efforts.

One important caveat to keep in mind: *there is no quick fix.* This curriculum is about stopping violence by dealing with its underpinnings. Some of you may have consulted this curriculum in hope of quick solutions for high-profile violence in your school or community. That violence is a major concern of the Making the Peace program. However, we feel strongly that interventions focusing on the headline topics of youth violence—gangs, guns, and drugs—while ignoring the social and economic underpinnings, are ineffective and temporary at best, and promote and continue the violence at worst. Because these topics are the deadly consequences of structural injustice—and because young people are scared by the same headlines that frighten us—we directly confront these topics in the classroom. Still, the structural injustice *is* the real issue at hand.

Violence prevention is different from standard academic coursework, and the teaching of violence prevention may require a few new techniques.

Teaching by Facilitating

Many of us were taught that as adults and teachers we are the authority; we have the information students need, and our role is to inspire students to learn what we already know about particular subjects. This information, and the power that accompanies it, was passed down to us and certified by colleges, superintendents, principals, and boards of education.

But in dealing with the issues of violence in students' lives—family and dating relationships, racism, male/female roles, drugs, sexuality—young people are the experts. Although they have misinformation, they also have the reality of their experiences and, collectively, lots of untapped knowledge. Their culture, language, relationships, families, and neighborhoods are different from ours now and when we were their age. What young people lack is a safe place to put their experiences and information together as a group and develop solutions to their problems. They may also lack a deeper conceptual framework within which to place and understand their experiences. To be effective, we as teachers must *facilitate* a group process of discovery and change.

As a facilitator, the teacher guides a process in which members of a community examine the climate of their community, notice where the community is breaking down, and become enabled to take charge in changing that climate. This process creates a *learning community*: a group of people who learn together how to analyze and take action to change and build their community. Where the issue is violence, a learning-community approach is essential for the following reasons:

Young people are a community

School is an enormous part of young people's lives, the place where they are socially sanctioned to be with others their age. Young people in a school form a community. Like any community, they have both explicit and unspoken rules of decorum. They have people who lead, outsiders, and the outsiders' own leaders. They reflect and act on what the larger communities around them pass on to them, good and bad. Much of their interaction is implicit and taken for granted. Teaching the prevention of violence requires us to bring the norms or rules of this community into focus for all of its members, enabling them to change the norms if they need to. Teaching geared toward the individual learner—in which each student is encouraged, motivated, and taught as if he or she were an isolated individual—is ineffective here.

Rather, by turning the classroom experience into a community-building experience, we enable young people to help each other to be safer and to work for justice. This enables them to turn peer pressure into peer alliance, and competition and fighting into cooperation and respectful problem solving.

Young people's community extends beyond the classroom

It is often assumed that the rest of students' lives should be kept separate from the classroom, as it only distracts from the curriculum. But these "distractions" have reached gigantic proportions. The daily gauntlet of decisions young people face in negotiating family life, cross-cultural and intergender relationships, sexuality, money, work, contacts with police, the presence of weapons, and simple survival in an adult-defined world is more complex and overwhelming than ever before. Especially where violence is involved, students' learning processes are affected by what they bring to school with them. Teaching must bring this larger community into view; the curriculum must be made relevant to students' lives.

Teachers have a complicated and difficult role as a part of the student community

Being a teacher is not easy. We live in a society that allots inadequate resources to its teachers and schools. Classroom size has increased, salaries and benefits have decreased, many schools are chronically underfunded, and the varied and immediate needs of students coming into the classroom place ever-increasing demands on teachers and school systems. To compound the problem, teachers are near the bottom of the educational hierarchy in terms of power, status, money, and influence.

Many of us enter the teaching profession with a vision of how we can inspire and affect students; with ideals of how schools, curricula, and teacher-student interactions could be. This vision is soon blurred and these ideals are set aside in the face of daily classroom maintenance, discipline and grades, and declining working conditions and safety in educational and youth-treatment systems across the country.

People who work with young people are at a critical social juncture. When a larger society is under stress or breaking down at certain points—and the violence in our communites is a visible sign of that breakdown—it most shows itself in the lives of young people. Clearly one of the social functions expected of teachers and other youth workers is the handling, management, or even the control of young people on behalf of the larger society—making teaching very much like "front line" work, under conditions that sometimes look and feel like combat.

To teach these issues, we must be prepared to examine not only how they affect our students but how they affect us. This will mean acknowledging to young people that we are part of their community, and sharing our experiences with them as well as listening to theirs. We will need to agree to be equal partners with them—and accept them as equal partners with us.

Only young people can make the peace with each other

Young people are vulnerable to violence—from other youth and from adults—because they have not been given the tools, skills, and resources to take care of themselves. As a result, the norms they set with each other expect and condone violence, and reproduce the cynicism, hopelessness, and despair of the larger society. As adult allies we can provide tools, skills, and resources, but we are peripheral to their community and cannot establish norms for them. Only they can change the norms of their society to ones in which violence is not tolerated and human dignity is honored.

Our experience at the Oakland Men's Project has been that young people are respectful when respected, caring when cared about, hardworking when allowed to participate in defining the work, and only manipulative and dishonest when manipulated and lied to. In other words, they are very much like us.

Young people have always been in the forefront of social change, leading movements against injustice, inequality, and violence—sit-ins and protests during the early civil rights movement; protests against apartheid in South Africa; antinuclear organizing in Germany; and pro-democracy struggles in China. They need us to work *with* them, not for them. We can't do it in place of helping them do it. Facilitating is not rescuing or protecting; young people need neither. They need support in taking leadership to address issues of violence and injustice.

So Who's in Charge?

You don't have to be an expert in the issues to facilitate this curriculum. In fact, we expect that you will learn a lot as you go through it with your students. The curriculum is designed to build a strong community response to violence. For that to happen, community members must first acknowledge the violence that is happening, then work together to stop it. This will require you to be a *true* leader, one who fosters other people's leadership.

Young people stop violence by taking charge and leading. What does it mean for young people to lead? Leadership in school is often highly valued by adults in areas of "desirable" behavior, such as cooperation, academic performance, and school spirit—and unrecognized or resisted when it doesn't promote, or competes with, our leadership. Leadership doesn't have to be a competition—our authority doesn't have to be threatened by the authority of young people. And there are many ways to be a leader.

Young people lead in the classroom and among themselves by setting standards and trends in the clothes they wear, the music they listen to, the nerve they show, the things they start, the attitudes they flaunt, or just the passion and concentration they pour into an activity. Youth we might find to be troublemakers are usually leaders in their own right—they just happen to be leading in directions we don't want to go. They often speak for other young people about the (ir)relevance of the direction in which we are leading. The role for the facilitators should be not to discourage leadership but to develop and widen it, to open it up for group analysis, definition, and widespread participation. Not everyone is a leader in the traditional sense, but everyone has valuable experience to contribute to help lead the group *as a group*.

Our highest image of leadership in this program is that *everyone* in the group leads. And your job as facilitator is to think of the group as a whole and to bring out or call out everyone else's leadership. This means helping young people recognize and value their own and each other's participation in the group, making enough room for them all to take part, and bringing them to the point where they insist on making room for each other. This means paying a lot of attention to the group process.

When you are facilitating and things are not going smoothly, you and everyone in the group can stop and ask, "What's going on?" Often you discover that neither where you were going with the process, nor where some of them were taking it, is where the group needs to go. You can collectively renegotiate, calling on everyone's help. Violence happens when people are separated, excluded, ignored, or set apart. Making the peace requires all hands. When you help make this happen, you are becoming an ally to young people.

Being an Ally to Young People

We call an *ally* someone from outside a particular group who acts to interrupt and prevent the violence affecting that group. It is especially supportive for an ally to foster the leadership of that group. As an adult you can be an ally to young people in just the same way men can be allies to women who are facing violence from men, or white people can be allies to people of color who are facing racial violence. What does being an ally require?

An ally listens.

An ally is present.

An ally opens doors.

An ally takes chances.

An ally gets support.

An Ally Listens

Young people are rarely listened to seriously. Their needs, concerns, fears, and desires are constantly overridden by the necessities of daily life and the agendas of adults. They often don't trust their own thinking; they have not found their own voice. Their experience is that adults have the right to speak first—sometimes the only right to speak at all. This "right" is exercised by us sometimes unwittingly, by simple presumption; sometimes purposely, with the best of intentions. Classroom convention often expects or requires you to exercise it.

Because adults seldom listen to young people, and often don't listen well to each other, young people often lack models of respectful, attentive listening—and, as a consequence, don't know how to listen well to each other. Listening to young people shows them that we take them seriously, and that what they have to say is important. It models how they can listen to each other with respect and care. It challenges the social training they receive that one group must dominate discussion. And it is a dramatic first step in reaching across the social and cultural barriers between and among adults and young people that foster violence.

An Ally Is Present

You can probably think of ways you needed someone to be there for you when you were young. Although their lives are different from ours, young people today need our presence in similar ways. They need adults who care, who respect and appreciate them, who encourage them without imposing values or styles on them. Young people need adults who are willing to be honest about the realities they face, including the difficult issues of family violence; drugs; sexuality; poverty; gender; and racial, religious, and other kinds of harassment and discrimination. Being present for young people does not mean we cannot set limits or confront abusive behavior when necessary. But *backing up young people to set the limits and to confront the behavior is the most profound kind of alliance.* Being present means taking the time to respond to the needs and situations that young people present to us.

Another aspect of this kind of support is trust. Trust young people to be 100 percent powerful—to be capable of making the best choices and the most effective decisions. Young people have consistently been told they are less than, too young, not smart enough, too immature. As an ally, let them know that you expect the best from them, that you hold them accountable, and that you don't need to take care of them.

An Ally Opens Doors

As an adult, you have a degree of power, authority, some privileges, and access to resources. You open doors when you provide resources to young people and help prepare them to recognize, assume, and handle power.

Young people, individually or in groups, often make poor choices about dealing with violence because they are overwhelmed by fear, pain, frustration, or anger; they lack information; or they do not understand the choices they have. You open doors by providing information, by confirming their experiences, and by passing on tools they can use to analyze and understand what is happening to them. You open doors by helping to define and provide choices, by introducing them to others who have things they need, by allowing them ample time to deliberate and decide, and sometimes by just getting out of the way and letting them do it.

An Ally Takes Chances

Taking chances means making some mistakes. Society has taught us that as teachers and, more generally, as adults, we should not make mistakes around young people.

But the fact is, nothing changes when no one takes a chance. We have to be bold, take chances, mess up, fix it, and try again. As long as we focus on not doing the wrong thing, we stay timid and ineffective. The white ally who is continually cautious about whether she is saying the appropriate thing around people of color, the male ally who is trying his best to do nothing that will appear sexist to women, use up their power in being careful. The challenge as an ally is to try everything you can, throw away what doesn't work, apologize if appropriate, and keep on trying.

An Ally Gets Support

Many of us were told as teachers that if we were inspiring, diligent, and persistent we could single-handedly change the lives of the young people we taught. Although we can make a difference in young people's lives, we cannot work with them alone and unsupported for very long without experiencing isolation, burn-out, cynicism, and ineffectiveness. Facilitating this curriculum is like any other work with young people: we need adult support to do it effectively. We need to find other adults to share our excitement, ideas, feelings, and problems; to support us through the difficult times; to celebrate our victories with us. In this sense, doing *anything* alone almost always continues the practice of individual isolation that permits violence to continue. And young people need to see us modeling the community building, support, problem solving, and success that is possible when people work together with care and respect to address common problems.

From whom do we get help? In general, it is not appropriate for adults to use young people for support. They are not prepared nor equipped to support us, and they have their own problems to deal with. They need us to be available to support them with our more extensive experience, social status, and resources.

It is true that young people regularly give adults lots of emotional support, and we are supported by working with them. But because they are dependent on adults—for food, shelter, clothing, approval, work, grades, and evaluations—their support cannot be given freely without the possibility of some threat or coercion behind it. Though we can appreciate it when it is given, we should never ask for or expect support from young people. However, unless we look to other adults for support, we will end up taking out our needs for support on young people.

Working with youth is difficult and often unrewarded. We can't do it well over time without solid support from other adults who also value young people and are working to be allies. Some of us are blessed with work environments where we enjoy strong support from other teachers, staff, administrators, parents, or friends. Many of us, though, have to establish such support for ourselves.

A good way to begin is to share this curriculum with another teacher, staff person, or parent. Get them involved early on in reading and discussing this material. Start building a nucleus of adults who can work together and support each other. Young people will see and be inspired by your model.

Assessing the Classroom Community

You will encounter many issues when facilitating this curriculum. The conditions in and around schools and students' lives throughout the United States are too varied to have one curriculum seamlessly fit the needs of every school. We will discuss a few major variations of those conditions below and point you toward some resources. However, the most valuable resources are your own initiative and creativity and that of the students and other adults around you. We encourage you to use the curriculum as it is presented, but to modify and adapt it with the input of young people as you proceed. If something is not working, ask each other why. This curriculum is a beginning, not an ending.

Space and Time

Community building is mostly an informal process, involving lots of open discussion, activity, and movement. To support this process, the physical environment must be flexible—adaptable to the social and emotional needs of the students and the varied activities of the curriculum.

The activities in this curriculum range from games, lectures, and role plays to small- and large-group discussions and group projects, sometimes in the space of a class period. During some periods, if conditions allow, students will be making a lot of noise; at other times they will be sharing personal experiences and require a respectful—and to some degree confidential—environment. A circle or semicircle of chairs will allow the community of young people to stay visible to and aware of each other, facilitating every student's participation. Moveable chairs enable you to adjust the scene easily to balance the weight of the discussion.

You can provide some continuing structure—some security underlying the process—by hanging posters (especially the Agreements poster) about the room, establishing space for particular projects, and, as much as possible, protecting the class from distracting noises, sound-system intrusions, and activities beyond the classroom door.

We have geared each session to take approximately one class period—between 40 and 55 minutes. However, with the inevitable interruptions in most classrooms, you will sometimes find that issues and activities from one session spill over into the next. What looks like a secure block of fifteen sessions on paper may get thoroughly reshaped by larger school contingencies.

For a topic as provoking as violence prevention, you will have to plan your periods well in advance and prepare your students. You will need to accentuate the Agreements in the curriculum, which call on all participants to be present and to take part. And you will have to prepare yourself emotionally to begin class as promptly as you can and to let it go when it's over.

If you are leading a youth group or special activity, you can modify the curriculum for a two- or three-day, six-hours-per-day workshop for a single group of young people. In our experience, longer periods—balanced by games, breaks, and physical activity—enable participants to get deeper into the issues and to form powerful friendships and alliances with one another.

Gender Issues

Most classrooms have an equal balance of young women and young men, and this curriculum is designed with that in mind. If there is a heavy imbalance of one gender, some adaptation of the exercises, especially in the sessions on gender, will be necessary.

More Men

If there are more men than women (or even if they are roughly equal in number), the young men sometimes drown out the young women. The climate in the group may already involve teasing, harassment, intimidation, or dismissal of the women, even if it looks like the boys are just kidding around. Young men often engage in put-downs of women as a way of trying to stay safe with each other. And even if young women are being harassed, they may feel they can't tell you because it would be betraying other young people to an adult. They may deny what's happening or try to protect the young men from you as a way of protecting themselves from the young men.

If you are male yourself, you may not see all the ways that young women can be silenced or invalidated. Consider cofacilitating the class with a female teacher. You might also want to check with the young women outside of class to see how safe they feel and what would increase their participation.

Whether you are male or female, it is your responsibility to question and challenge, rather than to collude with, the male bonding that occurs around sexism.

More Women

If there are more women than men, watch out that the young men do not become personal targets of the young women's anger about male violence; this just breeds defensiveness and silence in young men. Young men may already be insecure because they feel that women are better at conversing about relationships and feelings. Unchecked, this dynamic can also divide women from each other because some will want to stand up for the men. Keep the focus on understanding the issues, the feelings and experiences, not on blaming individuals in the class nor determining whether "all men" are good or bad. If valid confrontation does occur, use it as an opportunity for listening, increasing understanding, and building alliances.

Men Only

While designed for a mixed-gender group, this curriculum can also be used for a male-only group. Although the men will lack women's input, they will be able to talk in more depth about being male and dealing with violence than they might otherwise perceive as being safe. If you present the curriculum to a group of men, encourage them to explore the costs and effects of male socialization on themselves, their relationships with each other, and their relationships with women. Avoid talking about or blaming women in their absence. For further material on working with young men, see *Young Men's Work: Building Skills to Stop Violence* (Creighton and Kivel, 1995).

Women Only

If you work with a group of women only, take advantage of the lack of male presence to go into depth about female socialization, especially effects on body image and self-worth. You can also focus much more safely on the experiences of victimization and fighting back, and on the internalized sexism that trains women to mistrust and compete with each other.

Race Issues

Most schools in the United States are racially segregated, partly because we live in segregated neighborhoods. Ideally, this curriculum will be used with a multiracial class—but then, ideally, we wouldn't need the curriculum in the first place. If your school is composed of 70 to 80 percent of one ethnic group (including white), we would consider it effectively segregated, even if a particular class is racially diverse. Segregated neighborhoods and schools can be discussed and analyzed by the class as one effect of racism.

Your own understanding of racism in American culture will be profoundly shaped by your ethnic identity. A first step for each of us as facilitators is to examine our own feelings about and experiences of racism and to anticipate where—in the charged, unrehearsed process of a classroom discussion of racism—our own feelings or experiences may get in the way.

Predominantly or Exclusively White

One of the effects of racism is that most white students attend schools with few or no people of color. Their primary experience of people of other ethnic groups may be through textbooks, television, movies, and music. Much of their information comes from family and friends who may themselves have little contact with people of color.

The material on personal identity and family background in Sessions 6 and 7 is crucial for white students. It will enable them to break down the misconception that they have no ethnic identity—that they are simply "American" (and, by implication, that people with darker skin tones or other more "visible" ethnic heritages are therefore less American). One effect of racism is that white people devalue, or lose entirely, their own cultural and ethnic identities.

In many regions of the United States, people of color within the community are largely invisible to white people. There may be long-standing, stable communities of Asian-Americans, African-Americans, or Latinos. There may be Native American communities in the area, people of color who are migrant workers, or recent immigrant communities. Making these communities visible can help young white people understand the effects of racism. An investigation into how and why the school or neighborhood became segregated can be a valuable activity. Students can also look within the school at admission policies, textbooks, jokes, and student culture for examples of racism and ways to become involved in being allies to people of color. Although the primary form of violence in an all-white school will be white-on-white violence, don't gloss over the sections on racism because of a lack of people of color in the classroom. We are *all* affected by racism.

Predominantly or Exclusively People of Color

Some schools are almost exclusively African-American, Latino, or Asian-American; others have great ethnic diversity. Sessions 6 and 7 can, with a few adaptations, work well in all of these contexts.

Although a school may be predominantly, for example, African-American—perhaps including the teachers, staff, and administrators—there are probably still many problems related to race within and outside the school, including racially stereotyped textbooks, unequal urban and suburban funding, selective student discipline, police harassment, and tracking.

Nationally, the percentage of teachers of color is decreasing steadily; in schools having a majority of students of color, many of the teachers will be white. If you are a white teacher of students who are predominantly or exclusively people of color, you will need to look to your students for information about how racism affects their lives. You will probably be able to overcome any mistrust they have of you for being white by raising these topics, respecting their experience, and remembering that they are the experts. So that your own feelings won't prevent you from being there for your students, you will need to establish your own support system outside of the classroom. See *Uprooting Racism: How White People Can Work for Racial Justice* (Kivel, 1996) for resources for white teachers.

Adults, whether of color or white, are sometimes reluctant to talk about racism with a class of predominantly youth of color. Some of this may be subtle racism—the perhaps unconscious belief that this class is more "dangerous" than others. Well-meaning adults may also fear that students of color will use this topic as an "excuse" to rage, to be apathetic or hopeless, or to strike out. Usually the reverse is true: it is a relief to young people to have racism acknowledged. They cannot take full responsibility for making better choices unless they can discuss and analyze the constraints on their lives and community.

In classrooms that are racially diverse but predominantly made up of students of color, set aside time for young people of color to meet in ethnically separate groups to voice their concerns, anger, fears, and hopes. Emphasize that this is an opportunity to congregate—not to segregate—with the specific purpose of examining racism and its effects on their lives. They also need structured time to hear the ideas of members of other groups of people of color; one way that racism works is to pit one group against another. Such an occasion is not a time to figure out who has it the worst but how each group can be the best possible ally to the others. Ethnic pride, history, celebration, and alliance are all areas that students may identify and organize around.

Finally, without a good understanding of racism, young people of color are prevented from analyzing the dynamic in which the power-lessness, fear, and anger of racism is turned into violence against their peers and themselves. They have learned the same stereotypes about themselves that white youth have learned about them. You may be surprised about how deeply these messages of hopelessness and distrust of others have been set in place.

Racism is extraordinarily difficult to talk about in any classroom, especially when the talk involves personal experience and when the subject is the racially charged issue of violence. But the rewards are profound—as if a great secret had finally been divulged and reality let into the room.

Economic Class Issues

Economic issues are rarely talked about in relationship to violence, but they are clearly at the core of students'—and everyone else's—lives. Although most students attend schools that are segregated by class, even small differences in economic resources and opportunity can produce anger, frustration, despair, resentment, and violence among young people. Much male/male competition and fighting is related to real and perceived differences in wealth, employment opportunities, and overall status—and future possibilities for education, employment, and income. Drug dealing and fights over athletic shoes and jackets are related to money. Some young people even avoid coming to school because they don't have the "right" clothes or are ridiculed for shopping at secondhand stores; such training begins very early. When a young man's primary way of earning respect is to have the financial means—money to wear the right clothes, to drive the right car, and to manipulate other people, including girlfriends—perceptions of class easily lead to violence.

You are probably well aware of the economic circumstances of the community of students you teach—the unemployment rate, the types of jobs available, the standards of living—all of which have an effect on the way that violence is acted out among young people.

Members of wealthier communities tend to have the resources to keep much of the violence within the home and off the streets. Drug use, men battering their partners and children, child sexual assault, and suicide may not be as visible in these communities but may be taking no less a toll than in less affluent communities.

In poorer communities, because there are fewer present and future work options, economic pressures may make young men and women more desperate, less self-assured, and more cynical about the value of education. There may be more visible or dramatic incidents of violence or more media attention paid to them than in wealthier communities.

In either case, economic differences within a community can be the cause of—or used as justification for—various kinds of violence and harassment. Set aside your expectations. Listen to your students describe the kinds of violence they have experienced, and help them understand that the roots of much of the violence in our society lie in our economic system and the inequality, competition, scarcity, and consumer values it promotes.

In every community, people promulgate or accept the image of violence as a problem of the working class or the poor. This stereotyping is a form of violence itself, dividing low-income people from each other while silencing victims and licensing the violence among high-income people. Your role is to expose the relevant issues and help young people to explore them with one another.

Regional Issues

Some truths about gender, race, and economic class cross geographic lines. But differences of region and environment also affect culture, access to resources, and the experience of violence.

Young people in rural areas often lack age-appropriate community services and face declining work opportunities; isolation and poverty can trap young women in early childbearing and domestic abuse. These same economic hardships can send young people to cities, giving them less incentive to build community where they are. On the other hand, there may be great latent pride in the area's land and history, which you can call upon to reinstill a sense of community pride.

Urban environments offer more services *and* more vulnerability to street and neighborhood violence. In larger school systems, students may experience a greater variety of teaching materials and subjects, have more access to information, and meet teachers with different backgrounds—but more students get lost in the system. It is also more likely—because of economic segregation and racist law-enforcement policies—that students are confronting danger from drug dealing, gangs, police brutality, and weapons.

In suburban environments, young people face another set of circumstances: few places for young people to gather, economic segregation and isolation, high rates of invisible family violence, status built on achievement and conspicuous consumption, and the feelings of displacement suffered by people living in mobile, "developed" communities.

Violence by age, gender, race, and class cross these boundaries, and all young people need to discuss them. However, the focus of the discussions in this program is always the community you are in—how it fits, how it is different, and what must be done *where you are*.

Immigrants

If you are working with students from recently immigrated families, some of the violence they are dealing with will be related to language barriers, the stereotypes and prejudices of more established communities, the fear and harassment associated with immigration regulations and restrictions, and the lack of services and access to appropriate services for survivors of violence. Moreover, some recent immigrants

may have had experiences of war, rape, torture, assassination, forced relocation, or extortion in their countries of origin. Their first needs may be to deal with these previous experiences of violence, and there may be few resources available to them.

You will have to help nonnative English speakers understand the materials and participate fully in the discussions. They will probably have different cultural styles, different levels of comfort with public discussion of personal issues, and different fears about public participation from nonimmigrant students. And they have entirely unique experiences as mediators and interpreters between public officials and their families. Talk with other adults from their culture to open doors to this curriculum with them. Cofacilitate with people from the cultures represented in the class when possible. Immigrant students may need help finding their voice within the classroom. Always make time for them to speak up for themselves within the larger group discussion. At the same time, students whose first language is English may have to be challenged on their misconceptions of the cultures of immigrant students.

Other Considerations

Recent Violent Incidents

In many schools, this curriculum will be introduced, intentionally or not, after an incident of violence. It may have been a dramatic event, such as a drive-by shooting, an interracial fight, a student shooting, or a suicide. It may have been less dramatic but no less significant: a boyfriend publicly beating up his girlfriend, a rape of a student, the presence of guns in the school, charges of sexual harassment or racism brought against a teacher, ongoing police harassment of young people.

Even when they don't appear to notice, students are always affected by these events. Although abuse is a constant background factor in many students' lives, such events can trigger major emotional responses such as despair, fear, anger, and confusion. Within the curriculum, there are many opportunities for students to write about and discuss recent incidents of violence, both public and private. Healing from the effects of violence is important for each individual and can be a catalyst for students joining together to make the peace at their school.

If major trauma has resulted from a recent incident or series of incidents of violence on your campus, you may need to enlist the aid of professional and nonprofessional community counseling resources to help students heal. A public ceremony may help to reunite the community. As you use the curriculum, frame it in the context of what is currently happening. Allow young people many opportunities to talk about what is happening, how they feel about it, what kind of support they need from each other and from adult allies, and how they want to respond to the violence.

Gangs

Young people need to be able to hang out with friends where they feel safe. They need a forum in which they are respected and listened to; where they can make plans, talk about their lives, and make a difference, or just feel that they belong. The absence of such opportunities, coupled with deteriorating communities, inadequate schools, insufficient jobs, bleak future prospects, and daily violence leads to pressure on young people to join gangs. They may be looking for protection, validation, support, status, or economic opportunity. Through gang membership young people gain short-term respect, safety, excitement, and support. However, this is often at the cost of escalating levels of violence in their own lives and in the surrounding community. Faced with immediate danger and limited long-term options, many young people see few realistic alternatives to gang participation, despite the long-term cost.

When young people have opportunities in school or elsewhere in their lives to participate, to be respected and listened to, to support and challenge each other, to take on responsibility and do meaningful work, violence-based gangs will be less attractive. When communities provide jobs, education, and meaningful, social, cultural, and political partcipation, gangs will have little attraction. But these opportunities must be available to everyone—youth of color as well as white youth, poor youth as well as middle-class youth—or those left out will turn elsewhere to get their needs met, and that will likely be detrimental to themselves and their society.

There are a few programs for addressing gang violence directly. The Making the Peace curriculum addresses the root causes of violence and isolation in young people's lives through the mobilization and leadership of young people themselves so that gang participation will be neither inviting nor satisfying.

Guns

When you take up the subject of guns in Session 11, you are taking on one of the most high-profile issues affecting young people. This is also the issue, along with drugs and gangs, that teens have most often been told by adults to "just say no" to. Ironically, as with drugs, it is adults who produce, distribute, make available, profit from, and then blame young people for having guns. By raising the issue, you will invoke students' suspicion that they are about to be lectured to again. In addition, since the presence of weapons in general, whether in the classroom or at home, raises everyone's fears, this session may be doubly difficult to facilitate. But it is also a great opportunity.

Young people carry guns and other weapons to feel powerful and in control, and because they are afraid. Guns symbolize the power to control others, to get one's way, as well as the most visible day-to-day fear young people have: the fear of being hurt or killed.

The United States leads the world by many times in handgun ownership and adolescent death from guns. Guns and images of guns are present everywhere in American society, although they are more visible in some communities than in others. Many young people do not experience the direct presence of gun violence in their lives, but the number who do is increasing. The presence of a gun anywhere in a student's life can bring paralyzing fear and potential violence. How to deal with a physical fight, especially where guns are or might be involved, is often the first thing young people want to know when the issue of violence is raised.

No amount of metal detectors or other adult-based protective action will stop teen use and abuse of guns or make the environment completely safe. We need to help young people understand the dangers of arming themselves and to challenge the widespread thinking that using any kind of force to resolve conflicts is justifiable, even "in self-defense." When young people participate in creating a safer school community, they don't feel they need to carry guns to be safe and so can challenge those who do.

Your work with this issue will be more effective if you remember that the purpose of this session is not to lecture students about guns, but to help them think about how they are actually affected by guns in the community and how they can make practical decisions to keep themselves safe.

Homophobia

Homophobia—the fear of lesbians and gay men, the fear of being gay or of even being thought to be gay—is always at work on a school campus. You will encounter it wherever young men are together because it is part of the way the male role is enforced. This fear is also a basic provocation to violence. Call a guy a "wimp," "fag," or "sissy," imply that he is somehow less than a "real" (heterosexual) man, and he either has to fight to defend himself or hurt someone else to prove he is tough. We cannot lower the levels of male/male violence unless we are willing to talk about the fear that every man and young man carries with him. Some key ideas and realizations that will help make it safer for gay and heterosexual students alike are the following:

1. Everyone, no matter what their sexual orientation, has the right to be safe. No matter what your beliefs about other people, you have no right to commit violence against others.

2. Many young people are lesbian, gay, bisexual, or simply questioning their sexuality. They are present in all gatherings of youth, even if their sexuality is hidden, and even if it is hidden from themselves. This diversity is normal. It is also normal for young people to have questions, doubts, and strong feelings about their sexuality.

3. You cannot tell a person's sexual orientation from how they talk, act, look, or what other people say about them.

4. Young men are pressured by peers, parents, and the media to toughen up, to suppress feelings, to eliminate or hide certain aspects of themselves, and to fight and hurt other people to prove their masculinity.

5. An essential part of making the peace for young men and women is breaking out of the rigid gender-role boxes (explored in Sessions 9 and 10), treating everyone with respect, and eliminating gay-baiting (provoking a fight by calling someone a "fag" or the like) and gay-bashing from the school community.

6. As a facilitator, you should always assume that lesbian, gay, bisexual, or questioning youth are present—though you can never presume who is and *must not* compel anyone to so identify themselves. Never let a homophobic remark go unchallenged or unquestioned—and an important part of the lesson is that your students learn to do the same.

Reporting Family Violence and Sexual Assault

Attention to violence usually focuses on the most visible and dramatic instances of male/male fights, shootings, gang warfare, and, sometimes, suicide. However, the form of violence that the greatest number of students endure—often on a regular, long-term basis—is physical and sexual abuse within the family. Sexual and physical abuse in relationships outside the family, particularly in teen couples, is also much more common among young people than we might admit. One in four girls and one in six boys is sexually assaulted before the age of eighteen. Physical abuse of young people is endemic in many communities. Young women are routinely vulnerable to sexual assault and harassment on dates, on the streets, and at home. Even if you are in a school and community with little overt or public violence, you can be sure that young people are experiencing this kind of violence privately.

It is crucial to identify and focus attention on relationship violence, and you will find that young people cope with it in many ways. Some students will come forward with their own stories of abuse. While disclosure of abuse is not the goal of the Making the Peace program, it is not infrequent. If you make it safe enough, young people will tell you what is happening to them. You should be prepared to respond and to work out intervention where it is required.

Find out what the reporting requirements are in your state and how reporting is done. Discuss with your principal and other staff how to respond to young people in abusive situations. Make sure you have *planned for adult backup ahead of time* for this eventuality. Steer the young person to appropriate resources for support and intervention if necessary. Call your local rape prevention center, child assault prevention program, and battered women's shelter for resources in your area. *In every case,* talk with the student about what you are required to do and what support he or she needs and how to get it.

When someone tells their story publicly, the entire group is affected. The student may need a chance to talk about his or her feelings—and, if the person is asking for assistance from the group, to discuss how they can best support that person. This is not a time to talk about, gossip about, or blame the discloser; it is a time to remind everyone of the agreement of confidentiality.

Some students may deny the possibility that they could ever be victims of abuse. They may say things like, "I would never take it; I would fight back." Vulnerability to violence can be terrifying; denial is one way of dealing with that fear. However, it can also make these young people very critical of others who have experienced assault, blaming them for their victimization. It also creates an environment in which it is now unsafe to share cases of personal abuse; people who have experienced abuse are silenced by the response of their peers and can end up feeling isolated and unsupported in addition to blaming themselves for the violence that happened to them.

Given the pervasiveness of violence, no one is immune from possible sexual assault, robbery, or physical attack. It is at this very point—when we want to separate ourselves from the survivors of violence—that we need to recognize our common vulnerability and work to make it safer for all of us.

Because there is little public discussion of family violence and sexual assault, much confusion, misunderstanding, and fear surround these issues. Reading some of the resources listed on pages 173–76, talking with other adults, looking at and processing your own experiences, and modeling the five qualities of being an ally (see page 161) will help you facilitate these materials effectively.

Resistance from Students or Staff

Resistance is a normal part of any process of change. Beyond changing individuals, making the peace will require substantial changes in the ways we live together and the ways we have learned to see—and not see—each other. If you are effective with this material and students start to organize, take leadership, and confront the violence they ex-

perience, you may meet resistance, cynicism, or anger.

Resistance to change is most likely to come from people who gain or maintain some authority, power, and status by being abusive.

Some resistance will come from the students themselves. For example, some young men may resist facing how much violence happens to women; white youth can find it very difficult even to understand, much less accept, the concept of "no reverse racism" explained in the curriculum. It is best to face this resistance patiently and firmly, even welcome it. If young people believe that the group will work through resistances together, all will feel more entitled to contribute. At the very least, you can remind them of the agreement (explained in Session 2) that they don't have to agree with everything in the curriculum, just try it on.

There may be more troublesome resistance from outside the class—from students not exposed to the process, from other staff, and from families. Deep-seated patterns of violence or abuse in families, at school, or in the larger community are held in place by structural inequality and histories of injustice. It is not possible to deal with violence without experiencing conflict and encountering resistance. One goal of this curriculum is to enable your students and you to meet conflict and face resistance effectively.

It is important that you already have in place a community of support among staff and students when this occurs. To counter resistance effectively, you will have to assess its source, what it is really about, and your available resources.

The broader the base of participation and leadership you can accumulate, the less vulnerable to resistance you will be, and the more effective you will be in making the peace. And remember this: if you are meeting resistance, you have probably made a difference.

Preparing Yourself

Give yourself as much lead time as you can to schedule the course, to prepare yourself for leading it, and to line up cofacilitators, support people and friends with whom you can discuss the issues and prepare. Think about what kind of emotional readiness you will need for listening to and facilitating young people's dealing with violence. Presenting the course thoughtfully will require you to reexamine your own gender, racial heritage, age, economic background, and family history. How might the curriculum affect you? Which parts might require extra preparation because of the gender and racial dynamics between your students and you? How can you personalize the material by sharing your own history and culture? What other kinds of background reading, film viewing, or discussion with others might be useful to you?

Consider the rhythm and pacing of the course: how can you balance the light with the heavy—exercises, games, and group activities with deep discussion? To some extent, this curriculum works by bringing up or reminding us of painful experiences and feelings. You must remember to take care of yourself, to proceed at whatever pace you can, and to trust that you are doing your best.

In the week before you begin, let your students know what is coming. You might put up some of the Making the Peace posters and start arranging the chairs and having your students sit as they will during the course. If they are available, hang up pictures or quotations of people who have been on the front lines of waging peace, people who are admired and respected by your students. As a preliminary activity, have students informally survey the nightly news, magazines, and newspapers about local, national, or international conflicts involving violence or peaceful resolution of conflict, especially involving age, gender, race, or economic issues. You might hold a class discussion about young people's previous experiences of adults talking to them about violence or drug use. What do they remember? What was useful for them to hear? What wasn't?

Assessing Your Situation

The Making the Peace curriculum is designed to be used in a variety of school and other youth settings. The following questionnaire will help you to assess your situation and adapt the curriculum to your own needs.

1. In which of the following settings will you present the program:

   public school   private school   correctional institute

   religious program   community youth program

   drug program   residential program

2. Do you have support for the program from the following?

a. administrators	yes	no	mixed
b. staff	yes	no	mixed
c. parents	yes	no	mixed
d. youth	yes	no	mixed
e. community organizations	yes	no	mixed

3. Are there other adults from whom you can get support? List them.

4. Are young people allowed to have a voice in this institution? If so, in what ways?

5. Which of your students have leadership potential? Which have "nontraditional" leadership potential? List them.

6. Are there people whose support you need before you can begin the program? How can you get their support? (For example, by sharing these materials, through personal conversations, with the help of a community leader?)

7. What kinds of family, interpersonal, or neighborhood violence are your students dealing with that you know about?

   a. male/male fights

   b. female/female fights

   c. bullying

   d. lack of jobs and economic development within the community

   e. lack of money, resources, and support at school

   f. drive-by shootings or other street violence

   g. gangs

   h. drug use

   i. drug-related violence

   j. domestic violence

   k. child sexual assault at home

    l. sexual harassment within the school

    m. physical or sexual assault in dating situations

    n. suicide

8. In addition to this curriculum, what other resources do you have to work with?

    a. counselors, social workers, psychologists

    b. coaches and other recreation staff

    c. other youth programs

    d. conflict-resolution or mediation programs

    e. health clinics

    f. drug programs

    g. job-training programs

    h. active parent involvement

    i. active civic, religious, or business support

Ways to Continue Making the Peace

Once the class or group has finished the basic fifteen-session curriculum, there are many directions you and they can go. You are a valuable judge of what is possible given the young people you are working with. Sessions 13, 14, and 15 have already initiated some thinking on their part about what they can do personally and as a part of the larger community. What follows are some suggestions about possible follow-up activities.

Discussion and Study Groups

The group may simply want to continue the discussion and study begun in these sessions. They may not feel ready, well-enough informed, or united enough to take action. Let the students participate in deciding how to follow up the topics of the curriculum. Any issue presented during the sessions could be the focus of more in-depth discussion and exploration, perhaps employing historical topics, current events, more complex examples and problem solving, and more varied cultural activities.

Although further study should be encouraged, this is not meant to be an academic curriculum. The emphasis should remain on *applying what students learn to their own lives and relationships.* The following areas may make good follow-up topics. Any of these topics—or projects you develop—could be adapted to artistic, musical, written, or other creative expressions.

- What would it mean for a neighborhood, city, or country to be at peace?

- How have different peoples survived violence and resisted oppression?

- How is violence and resistance to it expressed through popular culture? Through classical culture?

- How do gender roles and gender-, racial-, and class-based inequality influence various aspects of American life? How are they played out differently in other cultures? What can we learn from this?

- Historically, how have communities organized to gain power? What struggles are occurring today that we can learn from?

- How and where have youth taken leadership in the fight to end violence and to create a more just society?

Support Groups

During the sessions, many issues might arise—such as violence-free relationships, sexual abuse survivors, staying drug-free, eating disorders and weight problems, and developing responses to violence—for which students or staff identify the need for a support group. Check to see whether students are interested in support groups on particular topics, perhaps by using the handouts supplied in Session 15. Find out what their needs are and who might be available and have the experience to lead the group. Sometimes support groups are co-led by an adult and a young person. Research and enlist the aid of support groups already in the community.

The Resources section at the end of the book can direct you to information sources that can guide you in setting up and running a support group. The last chapter of the book *Helping Teens Stop Violence*, by the authors of this curriculum, describes how to run a teen support group, complete with agendas, training guidelines, and useful forms for initiating, conducting, and documenting the group. *Feed Your Head*, the facilitator's guide by Earl Hipp, is also an excellent resource for facilitating a teen support group.

Advocacy Groups

An advocacy group is a support group whose members share a particular ethnic, racial, religious, class, gender, or other common denominator. The purpose of the group is not only support but advocacy for the concerns of that group within the campus or community. Such groups may remain primarily places for people to come together in a safe and supportive environment; others might identify issues on campus that the members want to advocate for or organize around. Advocacy groups usually function best when facilitated by an adult sharing the particular attribute or goal of the group. See the resources mentioned under "Support Groups" above.

Peer Education

Some students may want to share topics or issues in this curriculum with their peers or younger youth. To become peer educators, they will have to learn how to facilitate a group by working with an adult who can help train them to put aside their own needs and focus on the group process. See the resources cited under "Support Groups" above. If young people form a campus action group (see below), they will need to have a process to bring in and educate new members about the group's core issues. The more systematized this peer education process, the better it will work.

Conflict Resolution and Mediation

Some students want to intervene directly in violent incidents or start a peer conflict-resolution program. This is one way for them to take a more active role in reducing violence. There are many guides available for setting up such a program, and conflict-resolution programs are established throughout the country. There is probably already a school or school district near you that you can turn to for advice and information. A conflict-resolution program does not supplant the need for a continued use of this curriculum, because such programs do not focus on prevention and do not prepare young people to address the social causes of violence. However, they can be a important component of the Making the Peace strategy.

Campus Action

Some students may want to address immediate or long-standing issues by forming an action committee. An action committee focuses on a general topic area (sexual harassment, teen dating violence, fights, racism on campus) or responds to a specific, recent incident (a suicide, a drive-by shooting, a major fight). In either type students should be encouraged to analyze the causes of the violence, plan out strategic actions, and mobilize other students in support of their plan.

Days of Respect Program

The *Days of Respect Organizer's Manual*, a companion part of the Making the Peace program, offers students, parents, and teachers guidelines for a schoolwide campaign focused on respect and violence prevention.

Community Action

Sometimes campus-initiated groups will decide to address issues in the larger community. Students may want to get involved with school-district issues such as youth representation on the school board, guns and violence prevention on campus, and textbook reviews and multicultural curricula. They may want to work with community-based organizations involved with projects of economic development, recreation, toxic dumping, police review, health care access, racism, or violence in the media, to name a few.

Resources

The many resources listed on pages 173–76 are a good source of support and further ideas. In particular, our previous book, *Helping Teens*

Stop Violence, provides an in-depth look at the violence and equity issues presented in this curriculum. Earl Hipp's *Feed Your Head* is a practical guide for facilitating groups for young people. The Oakland Men's Project is also available for consultations and training—see our address and telephone number on page ii at the front of the book. If you have any final doubts or questions, give us a call.

■ ■ ■

Students have the capacity to identify and plan actions around the issues they feel are important. However, they need a lot of support in setting up leadership, education, planning, and implementation. On the other hand, adults can bog them down in meetings, presentations, reports, and other "adult" ways of thinking and acting. We need to help them develop leadership skills without diminishing their initiative and creativity.

In any project where young people work with adults, it is easy for the adults to take over because of their expectations of being in charge and because of young people's internalization of negative messages from adults. Pay attention to keeping young people in the forefront of the project, supporting not just the few who are articulate and most self-assured, but all the young people involved. You may, at times, have to challenge other adults who are dominating the space and time of the group or who are disrespectful of the young people. Of course, that's what being an ally to young people is all about.

We've just suggested a few of the ways that young people might take this curriculum and move forward with it. The Oakland Men's Project is available for technical assistance in implementing the curriculum and doing follow-up. Share your successes with us and ask for our support when you need it. Working together with young people, we can *make the peace.*

The Roots of Violence

Session 1 introduces a definition of violence and helps students develop a vision of safety and respect. Session 2 discusses the origins of violence and introduces basic classroom agreements that will be used throughout the program. Session 3 explores the roots of violence in institutionalized injustice: connections are made between social injustice and interpersonal and self-destructive acts of violence, and the "cycle of violence" is explored. Session 4 introduces the concept of being an ally to others to stop violence and presents the Ally Pledge. Session 5 looks at the abuse that young people face—adultism—and explores how young people can be allies to each other.

Making the Peace

Aims

- To give an overview of the Making the Peace program: what violence is, how it affects us, and how we can make the peace

- To set the tone for the fifteen sessions: getting to know each other, looking at our relationships with each other, becoming stronger allies, building community

- To begin to explore and create safety

Skills

Students will

- Understand and use a working definition of *violence*

- Identify several ways violence affects them

- Identify the need for and the value of creating a safe place/class

Preparation

- You will need copies of Handouts 1 and 2 and On Your Own sheet 1. You will also need butcher paper, markers, and tape.

Overview of the Session

In your own words, convey the following:

During the fifteen sessions of this class, we will be exploring how to make the peace. We will look at the ways we are not safe in our lives, and we will explore what we can do as a class and as a community to make the world a safer place, for all of us—at school, at home, and in our neighborhoods.

When I say the word violence, *what are the **first** thoughts that come to your mind?*

As students call out their ideas, list them on the board. Title the list "Violence."

In this class, we will look at many of these ideas, and more. We will be talking about some difficult issues, like violence, fighting, sexual and physical abuse, and racism.

When you are affected by violence, it feels very personal. It's not easy to talk about or even think about. To work on this together, we need to create some safety right away, so all of us will feel comfortable enough to take part. Today we will start by talking about what it means to be safe and what violence is; then we will take some first steps toward making the peace.

There are a few important things for you to know before we start. First, no questions are off-limits. Everyone has the right to ask questions about things that aren't making sense. Second, when we are talking about violence, everyone's feelings and thoughts are important; to make the peace, we need to analyze all the reasons for and responses to violence that you have experienced—we need to make sure that everyone participates.

Finally, I will often ask you to tell us as much about what you have experienced and what you think as you feel safe to do—I want us to stay focused on what's really happening in your lives. If you share with us something that is happening now—particularly in your family or in a personal relationship—where you or someone you know is being hurt, or you are hurting yourself or someone else, we will help you get help so that the abuse can be stopped. If the violence is something I have to report to others, I will let you know that and talk with you about how best to do that.

Now, let's take a minute for any questions you have so far.

Introductions

Tell students they will now practice listening to one another with full attention. Have a few volunteers tell about how they know when someone is really listening to them—and when someone isn't.

Divide the class into groups of five. Ask all group members to say one way they want the world to be safer for another young person or for themselves. For example, "I want parents not to hit their children for myself and my brother and sister," or "I want it to be safe on the streets when my friends and I walk home from school." Remind everyone to practice listening with full attention. Give them four minutes for this exercise, then recapture their attention.

Next, ask each student, speaking to the others in the small group, to finish this sentence three times: "If you really knew me, you would know that . . . " For example, "If you really knew me, you would know that I come from a large family and we're all really close," or "If you really knew me, you would know that I'm really a shy person but I like to party with friends." Give the groups three to four minutes for this exercise, then refocus their attention as a whole group.

Safety Visualization and Discussion

Tell students that you will now ask them to visualize something in their minds. Have them sit comfortably in their chairs, relax their bodies—close their eyes if they wish—and picture a place in the world where they feel completely safe. Invite them to stay with the first picture that comes to mind. The place they visualize might be at home, at a friend's, in the woods, or at the beach; it might be with someone or by themselves. Remind them that it is a place where they feel completely safe and unafraid.

Think about what it feels like to be in this place. Look around. What does it look like there? How does your body feel? What makes this place safe?

*This is a place where you can go in your mind when you need to feel safe. This is a sanctuary for you. A **sanctuary** is a place—like a temple, a church, a sacred space, or a shelter—where you are protected from anyone or anything that might hurt you.*

End the visualization by asking students to return to the classroom, to look around and feel themselves completely in their bodies again, ready to continue.

Have a few volunteers describe their sanctuaries. Ask others to describe what feelings they had during the visualization.

Ask the group to reflect for a minute on how they would be different if their real environment were perfectly safe for a day. How would they feel, what would they do or not do, where would they go? Alternatively, ask some students to share their completion of this sentence: "If it were perfectly safe, I would/could . . . "

Explain Handout 1, Personal Safety, and give students a few minutes to write a few ideas after each question. If they need help getting started, prompt them with a few questions. For example: Would having a gun make your home safer? Would an end to drug dealing make school safer? Remind the group that *all their writing in this class is for their eyes only;* it will not be handed in.

Ask students to share some of their ideas as you record them on the board near the earlier list on violence. Summarize by adding the title "Peace" to the list.

Working Definition of Violence

Refer to the "Violence" list made at the opening of the session.

This, among other things, is what threatens the peace and our safety.

Present this working definition of violence from Martin Luther King Jr.:

"Violence is anything that denies human integrity, and leads to hopelessness and helplessness."

Pass out Handout 2, What Is Violence? Ask students to jot down anything that counts as violence under this definition.

Closure

Ask students if there is anything they want to add to the "Violence" list on the board. Explain that stopping the violence on this list is the goal of the Making the Peace program.

Distribute On Your Own sheet 1, My Experience of Violence, and explain that students should take some time between now and the next session to answer the questions on the sheet.

On this sheet, you will write about a time that you experienced or witnessed violence. Briefly describe what happened and how it affected you. Bring this sheet to the next session.

What if . . .

Some students are disruptive? Ask these students what they need in order to be able to participate without disrupting others. Ask a few other students how safe they feel participating with the disruptions. Engaging the students in a discussion with each other about the issue will help them replace disruption with discussion and problem solving.

After each question below, briefly describe what you would need to be physically and emotionally safe. How would you need people to treat you? How would you need people to change how they act?

What would you need to be safe at home?

What would you need to be safe at school?

What would you need to be safe in your neighborhood?

What would you need to be safe at work (if you work)?

Complete this sentence: If it were perfectly safe, I could . . .

"Violence is anything that denies human integrity, and leads to hopeless-ness and helplessness."

— Martin Luther King Jr.

Write down anything that you think counts as violence according to this definition.

Describe a time when you were hurt, or saw someone else being hurt. What happened?

What did you do about it?

In what ways does this experience still affect you?

What Violence Is

Aims

■ To introduce a theory about human development that will help students understand themselves better

■ To establish ground rules for the Making the Peace sessions

Skills

Students will

■ Recognize effects of the social mistreatment of young people

■ Establish participation guide-lines (the Agreements), which will be in effect for the duration of the course

Preparation

■ You will need copies of Handouts 3 and 4 and On Your Own sheet 2. You will also need butcher paper and a marker or a chalkboard and chalk, and the poster of the Agreements or a transparency of Handout 4.

To Begin

Briefly recap the last session, especially for any newcomers. Ask for students' reflections on the On Your Own writing and the first session's material.

Overview on the Origins of Violence

Review Martin Luther King Jr.'s definition: "Violence is anything that denies human integrity, and leads to hopelessness and helplessness."

To make the peace, we have to begin looking at what violence is, where it comes from, and why it happens—not just the fights and beatings and homicides you hear about or see on the news, but what's behind them. Why does so much violence happen to children and teenagers, to women, to people of different ethnic and racial groups, to poor and working people?

It doesn't start this way. No one was born wanting to get their way by hitting others. No one was born wanting to beat, humiliate, or blow someone else away. Let's start at the beginning.

The Heart Exercise

Complete this exercise on the board or distribute Handout 3, The Heart Exercise.

Draw a large heart on a sheet of butcher paper or on the board. Tell students this is a portrait of a baby at birth. Have them call out words to describe a baby when it is born ("innocent," "sweet," "dependent," "noisy") and write them in the heart.

innocent
sweet
dependent
noisy

Next, have students call out what adults sometimes say to babies and children when the adults are irritated or angry ("shut up," "you're just a kid," "do what you're told"). Include what adults say when babies are acting in some of the ways inscribed in the heart ("grow up," "don't be so naive," "stop whining"). For every negative remark recorded, make a slash mark across the heart.

(If the exercise is bringing lots of responses, ask other questions. What gets said to children who are girls? To children whose skin is darker than "white"? To children who speak English in any way other than narrow "basic English" or who have an accent? To children with large bodies? A limp? A stutter? Continue to make slash marks as the remarks are thrown out.)

Human beings bruise very easily. Each of these words and remarks leaves a bruise. Each bruise develops a little scar. By the time we're adults, we have lots of scars.

Draw three or four concentric arcs over the scarred heart.

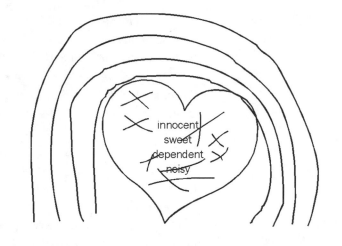

What else happens when a person gets a scar? That person tries to keep herself from being hurt the next time. She puts up a shield to protect herself. One shield for every scar. When a young person puts up many shields, it makes it very hard for the heart to grow. It becoems frozen in place, holding up all of its shields.

Referring to the remarks students previously called out as examples of what adults say to babies, have students call out particular behaviors—shields—a young person learns to use to protect himself from getting that particular scar again. For example, if an adult tells a young person to shut up, that person might learn to be silent all the time around adults; being told "you're just a kid," a young person might learn either to act very young all the time, or alternatively to act very mature and never let himself appear his own age.

Draw another heart, with lots of "scars" and "shields," next to the original.

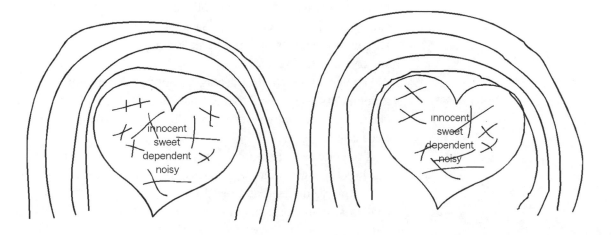

Now when two people meet, it's very difficult for them to see each other through all of their shields. Each finds it very hard to see the real person behind the shields, much less let themselves be seen. When you say something to me, it has to go through all your shields before it even gets out, so it may come out sounding different from what you intended. Then it has to get through all my shields, so by the time I hear it, it doesn't sound anything like what you intended. We often start fighting just because we have both been bruised so much and hold up so many shields that we don't know how to talk to or listen to one another.

Remember, our old shields can keep us from growing. They might be helpful sometimes, but we need to be able to put them down. Every time you can safely put a shield down, there's that much room for your heart to grow.

Take a few minutes to have students think or write about the questions on Handout 3. They can refer to their filled-out On Your Own 1 for ideas. As a class, discuss specific ways people can be affected by these bruises.

Before students begin to talk more openly and freely about their experiences of violence, help the class establish some ground rules that everyone will follow during the Making the Peace sessions.

The Agreements

Convey the following in your own words:

Our first step in this course is to make the peace with each other: to take down our shields. I'm going to ask you to try something: to make some agreements with me and the rest of us about how we will act around each other while we talk about violence. When we're working together on a hard topic, people may get upset, sad, or angry. Some may stop talking; some may start talking a lot. Let's talk about some agreements that can help all of us feel safe enough to keep participating and get each of our voices heard.

To introduce the Agreements to the group, you can explain the Agreements first, then display the poster or the transparency you made and distribute Handout 4, The Agreements, or do the reverse. Either way, talk about each agreement briefly, making sure everyone understands it, and ask students to raise their hands if they feel they can make this agreement. To save time you may want to run through all the agreements and then ask for anyone who cannot agree to the set to raise their hand.

When you reach the last agreement, ask students what additional agreements they need to feel safe enough to fully participate in the class. List their suggestions on the board, asking for clarification if necessary.

If anyone feels uncomfortable committing to a particular agreement, modify the agreement as a class until everyone can agree to it. Remind the students that they don't have to fully agree with everything that is said in class; they are only committing to "try on" the ideas.

If you haven't already done so, distribute Handout 4, The Agreements, and talk about the process of following them in class.

None of us will remember to keep the Agreements all the time, and some of them are really tough to keep. When someone forgets or is ignoring a particular agreement, that person needs to be gently and respectfully reminded. For instance, it's easy to forget to use "I" statements. A simple reminder from someone, and I can repeat what I just said using an "I" statement.

Talk with the class about some of the less obvious ways people can make others feel uncomfortable.

We have all learned many ways to put other people down, including subtle ways. What are some of the subtle ways this can happen in a classroom? (Facial expressions, noises, sarcastic comments, hand gestures, distractions, inattention, side conversations, eating, reading, for example.) Part of keeping the Agreements is being aware of the subtle ways we and others may be disrespectful and gently reminding each other that such behavior makes it less safe for everyone.

Closure

Allow students time to reflect on what the class has learned so far. Ask questions to encourage them to share their thoughts.

- How does this process feel after two sessions?

- What thoughts do you have about safety and violence?

- What might sabotage our abiding by the Agreements?

- What pressing issues do you want discussed during these sessions?

- Is there anything you've learned or thought about already that makes you want to change how you treat people or how other people treat you?

In preparation for Session 6, distribute On Your Own 2, My Family Tree. Explain that you are distributing this now because students will need some time to fill it out. Answer any questions they have about doing a family tree.

If possible, designate a space in class where students may display photos or other objects of their family history to share with the class; ask a couple of students to be in charge of organizing the display. You may want to clear a bulletin board for hanging students' family trees, and contribute your own family tree and photos or objects from your family's history.

Display the Agreements poster, or a paper copy of it, during all remaining sessions.

Draw a heart below, and write words in it that describe for you the qualities a baby is born with.

Now, draw "bruise marks" on the heart with words on them that describe things that get said or done to children that hurt or limit them.

In your life, how have you been bruised?

How has it affected you?

How might you have passed that hurt on to others?

Now, draw "shields" around the heart with words on them that describe shields you have developed to protect yourself. Which shields would you most like to get rid of and never have to use again?

To help make the peace, I agree to:

1. Respect others   I agree to give everyone respect, including myself. This includes being here—physically and mentally—when everyone else is here.

2. Listen to others   I agree to listen to others and to expect that others will listen to me. One person will talk at a time, without interruptions, and no one will monopolize the conversation.

3. Keep confidentiality   I agree to keep what is said in class or discussions confidential. I won't repeat what someone else says without getting that person's permission.

4. Offer amnesty   I agree not to blame, or "get back at" later, anyone for what he or she says. *Exception:* If someone says that he or she is being hurt now, or is going to hurt someone else or himself or herself, I will try to get that person some help.

5. Use put-ups, not put-downs   I agree not to put down, make fun of, or attack other people. I will not put myself down either; for example, I will not begin speaking by saying something like, "This may sound stupid, but . . . "

6. Avoid crosstalk and piggybacking   I agree to allow everyone to say what they need to say without debating, denying, attacking, *or* agreeing with or supporting it. I will allow people's words to stand on their own, without trying to take them over.

7. Allow the right to pass   I agree that everyone has the right to be silent when they want to be.

8. Respect feelings   I agree to respect and allow other people—and myself—to experience feelings of hurt, sadness, boredom, anger, and excitement.

9. Use "I" statements   I agree to speak only for myself and my own experiences. I will try to use the word *I* in place of the words *you, we,* or *they.* (This is a very difficult agreement to keep, but crucial. It helps us to speak about what is true for us and understand how each person feels.)

10. Try on the process   I agree to try on the process—these agreements and the ideas in this class—and I realize that in trying it on, I am not required to agree with it or accept it.

11. Take care of myself   I agree, as much as possible, to take charge of my own needs. This includes enjoying and having fun during the process.

. . . and to these additional agreements, which the group has decided on:

Starting with yourself, draw a family tree going back as far as you know or can find out about. Fill in the names of all the people you can, noting the jobs they did, where they lived, when they arrived in this country, and anything else you would like people to know about your family background. If it is part of the class project, bring in photos or other objects from your family history to share.

Sample Family Tree

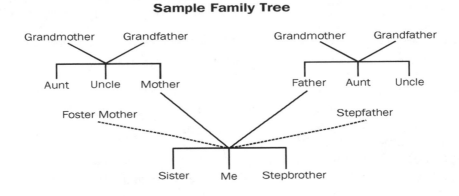

The Roots of Violence

Aims

- To introduce the idea that interpersonal violence has roots in structural social inequality

- To explore the concepts of oppression, internalized oppression, resistance, and alliance

- To begin building alliances among students

Skills

Students will

- Identify groups socially stratified into positions of power and positions of nonpower

- Locate themselves within more powerful/less powerful groups

- Trace the cycle of violence

- Define *oppression, internalized oppression,* and *resistance*

- Identify violence caused by oppression and violence caused by internalized oppression

Preparation

- You will need copies of Handout 5 and On Your Own sheet 3. You will also need butcher paper, markers, tape, and a transparency of Handout 5 (optional).

To Begin

Review of the Agreements and the Heart Exercise

Go over the Agreements briefly, and then ask students to review the Heart Exercise from the last session. If students seem receptive, ask for any further reflections on what has been discussed so far.

The Power Chart Exercise

Begin this exercise by explaining that you will be presenting a way to think about where much of the violence in our society begins.

Some of the bruises we get are deep. Some are systematic, coming at us all of our lives because of who we are, where we come from, what language we speak, what race we are, and what sex we are. Differences in gender, racial and ethnic heritage, age, physical ability, class, religion, and sexual orientation—whether visible or invisible—separate us into groups: usually one group of people who have some power or privilege over another group.

All our interactions take place in this social system of power. Not power from within, but power over. Not individual power or inner strength—we all have that—but power that is part of the everyday institutions of a society: the laws, the government, the justice system, the economic system, the education system, religious organizations, and the family. In all of these areas, one group has more than another; one group controls more than another.

Sample Power Chart

Power	Nonpower
Adults	Young people
Whites	People of color
Men	Women
Rich	Poor
Bosses	Workers
Gentiles	Jews
Christians	Non-Christians
Heterosexuals	Lesbians, gays, bisexuals

Draw the Power Chart on the board, display a transparency of it, or distribute Handout 5. You may want to write down the list first without the headings, and ask students what the two columns are about before writing the headings. Or, call out each pair of entries in the chart as a question ("Who has more power, adults or young people? Whites or people of color?") and then write the names in the appropriate columns.

Explain that you are using the term *people of color* to refer to all people who are not considered white in the United States, including African-Americans, Arab-Americans, Asian-Americans, Southeast-Asian-Americans, Latinos, Native Americans, and Pacific Islanders. Expect some questions or resistance about some of the categories; some students may have a hard time being tagged as part of a "power" or "nonpower" group.

Once the entire Power Chart is displayed, talk about what it reveals.

In our society, the groups on the left side of the Power Chart are allowed more power than the groups on the right. For the most part, they have better-paying jobs and better housing, education, physical security, legal protection, police protection, health care, and representation in government.

Of course, this isn't true for every individual in each group; there are always exceptions on both sides. But overall, the groups on the left have power at the expense of other, less powerful groups, whose access to such resources is limited or denied. These "nonpower" groups are often the targets for violence from the power groups. We might also call them the "target" groups.

Go down the list on the nonpower side, and ask for examples of the violence done to people in those groups—any ways that members of those groups undergo the "denial of human integrity." Write the examples to the right of the chart. Label this new list "Examples of Violence."

This is where all—or almost all—of the violence we are here to talk about comes from in the United States: the imbalance of power between groups of people.

The Cycle of Violence

Allow students several minutes to write down (or circle on Handout 5) where they fit on the Power Chart in each category. If someone is unsure where he or she fits in a particular category, ask that student to reflect on how he or she is seen by the larger society and to write *that* category down, along with any reasons he or she has for feeling uncertain.

Ask students what they notice about where they "belong." Make sure everyone realizes that they fit in groups in both columns. Some groups they always inhabit; others, like adult and child, they may move between.

Children who grow up in our society learn that some people are on the inside and some people are on the outside. We learn to stay out of the "one-down" groups as much as we can by finding groups on the "one-up" side to associate with. When power is distributed like this, we learn to try to survive at all costs, including passing on our pain by being violent to someone who is even more vulnerable than we are. We create an ongoing cycle of violence.

Think of the list you made of how young people are scarred. What is a young person who gets scarred learning about how to get and retain power in a society like this? Depending on a person's gender, race, economic background, and age, where will she or he go to get some power or social authority? What might she or he do?

Anatomy of the "Isms"

Explain to the group that when violence comes at a nonpower group from a power group, we call it *oppression*: oppression is when mistreatment and discrimination go from the power side to the nonpower side. What's most important to understand is that *oppression is impersonal.* It's part of the way our society is set up. No one necessarily intends to oppress anyone else.

We can call the power groups' oppression of the nonpower groups the "isms."

Have students review the first four or five lines of the chart, calling out the "ism" (racism, sexism, adultism) attached to each pair of power and nonpower groups.

Oppression is happening all the time, every day. And it isn't just "violent" violence, but also the discrimination that goes on day after day, separating people into different schools and different neighborhoods and different jobs—so much that we may not even consciously notice it.

All of the institutions in our society—government, the economy, the justice system, the education system, the church, and the family—help keep oppression going over and over again. These institutions pass on to us as children (indicate the "young people" slot on the Power Chart) that this is the way it is. They teach us stereotypes about each other, especially about people in "those" groups (refer to the nonpower groups), and they teach "those" people (refer to power column) to not even be aware when oppression is happening. We may even learn to blame "those" people (refer to nonpower groups) for what happens to them.

Have students call out examples of how members of the first three or four nonpower groups get blamed for what happens to them. Or, convey the following:

Instead of seeing men as being responsible for rape, we may talk about how women "ask for it" by manipulating men or dressing provocatively. Instead of seeing business owners as being responsible for low pay and dangerous working conditions, we may say that workers are lazy, untrained, or unwilling to work. Instead of seeing adults as being responsible for poor, overcrowded schools, we say that students are unruly, not smart enough, undisciplined, or have low self-esteem. This system of blaming the survivors of violence leads to what Martin Luther King Jr. called "hopelessness and helplessness."

No Reverse "Isms"

Take a few minutes to make the following distinction. With this definition of oppression, it doesn't make sense to speak of reverse "isms"—for example reverse sexism (systematic mistreatment of men) or reverse racism (systematic mistreatment of white people). Be very clear that, of course, violence, mistreatment, and stereotyping *is* done to members of power groups by members of nonpower groups (we call that *retaliatory violence*). What is different about oppression is that the *system* of power—including police, courts, housing, health care, and jobs—stays on the side of the power groups. Nonpower groups do not have the social power and command of resources to limit the powerful or to protect themselves from system-wide violence.

Internalized Oppression

Explain that another major source of violence comes from people on the nonpower side *internalizing* the oppression that is done to them.

People on the nonpower side eventually begin to listen to, and internalize, the lies and the stereotypes that the dominant group continually bombards us with. As we blame ourselves, we feel isolated, separate, and distrustful of others. We may come to believe that others in our group are to blame and that we deserve violence. We may come to feel frustrated, angry, and worthless ourselves. We may even lash out at individuals in the more powerful group (retaliatory violence), but this is usually punished quickly and severely.

When we internalize oppression, we generally take out our hurt in three ways:

1. against members of other nonpower groups

2. against other people in our own group

3. against ourselves

Ask students for examples of each of these three kinds of violence from several nonpower groups, including the "young people" category—examples of young people taking out hurt against other nonpower groups, against other young people, and against themselves. ("Violence against ourselves" might include unsafe drug use, unsafe sex, overeating, starving, self-mutilation, and suicide.)

All of these forms of violence that you have mentioned keep the system of power and control in place.

Effects of the "Isms"

This three-part exercise explores how the interconnection of "isms" affects real people, who of course occupy slots on both sides of the Power Chart. Focus students on how the people in each part of the exercise might contribute to the cycle of violence.

- You have talked about how each nonpower group is affected by violence. Pick *two nonpower groups* (for example, "young person" and "woman"). How is someone who is both young and a woman affected by oppression and internalized oppression?
- Now, pick *two power groups* (for example, "rich" and "white"). How is someone who is both rich and white affected by (protected from) oppression and internalized oppression?
- Now, pick *a power group* from one line and *a nonpower group* from another (for example, poor + man). How is someone in both of these categories treated? How does his *nonpower* status affect his place in his power group? How does his *power* status affect his place in his nonpower group? (For example, a man who is poor may be treated as a less successful man than a rich man, but as a poor person he may command more status and have more options than a poor woman.)

Resisting Oppression

Talk with the group about the idea that people use many ways to resist being mistreated.

No one asks for mistreatment. No one likes it. Remember the heart we drew: underneath the scars is someone who is good, honest, smart, brave, and stands up for what is right. All of us have resisted mistreatment, even if only by saying no in our minds.

Return to the Power Chart, and have students call out ways they know that individuals or groups in nonpower categories have resisted mistreatment from power groups. This may include individual actions such as women fighting back against sexual and physical assault, or social movements such as the civil rights movement, the women's movement, and neighborhoods organizing against police brutality.

Visualization

Explain that you would now like the class to participate in another visualization, and ask them to get comfortable. Ask the students to silently pick a nonpower group from the chart that they are currently a member of—the first one they think of when you give the direction.

Think of a time when, as a member of that group, you were a victim of violence of any kind from the power group—when you were yelled at, pushed, called a name, hit, discriminated against, or ignored. Stay with the first memory that comes up. Take a moment to re-create that scene.

Think about how that experience affected you at the time. Were you blamed in any way for what happened? Is there any way in which you blamed yourself?

Now, think for a moment of any way that you resisted. (Even saying no in your mind is a form of resistance.)

Now, think of any way that this experience still affects you.

Bring students' attention back to the classroom.

Closure

As a class or in small groups, have students talk for a few minutes about their thoughts and feelings. If they want to, they may share their stories or identify the nonpower group they chose.

Distribute On Your Own sheet 3, and respond to any questions students have about it. Remind students to keep working on their family trees for Session 6.

What if...

Some students quarrel with the Power Chart? If some students don't accept the Power Chart—for example, if a male student says women really have more power than men, or if a white student says he was beat up by three African-Americans and thus they have power over him—emphasize that we are talking about social power, not individual strength. Remind students of the difference between *oppression,* which is a system of power and control, and *individual acts of violence,* which are a response to oppression.

Point to the composition of Congress, the Supreme Court, corporate directors, and stockholders. Point to the disparity in wages among different groups. It may be useful to have several statistics, examples, or personal stories about how oppression operates as a system.

Yes, a person of color might beat up a white person. Ask the questioner to identify what kind of violence this is. If the police came, if the altercation went to court, or if the media covered it, how would the two people be treated? What difference does social power make in such a confrontation?

Power	Nonpower
Adults	Young people
Whites	People of color
Men	Women
Rich	Poor
Bosses	Workers
Gentiles	Jews
Christians	Non-Christians
Heterosexuals	Lesbians, gays, bisexuals
Able-bodied	People with disabilities
Teachers	Students
People born in the U.S.	Recent immigrants
Adults	Elder adults

Violence from power groups against nonpower groups, or *oppression,* leads to retaliatory, peer, and self-destructive violence. Each form of violence perpetuates the others.

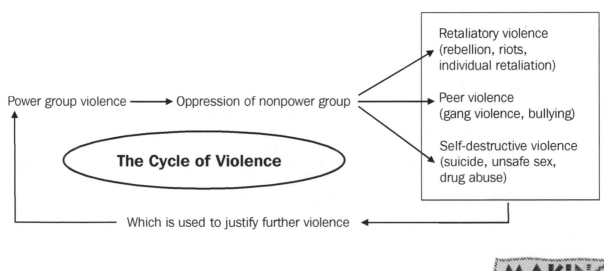

Think of a nonpower group of which you are currently a member. Write down the name of this group. Describe how your group has been hurt by a power group and what rights or resources have been denied to your group.

What are some ways members of your group have learned to attack each other? (For example, by putting down people in your group, competing, or fighting.)

What are some ways members of your group have blamed themselves or used self-destructive violence? (For example, by suicide, extreme dieting or overeating, self-mutilation, or heavy drug use.) Use examples from your school or neighborhood.

How have members of your group resisted mistreatment individually and as a group? (If you aren't sure, ask others in your group.)

What do you want members of the power group to know about you or your group?

Becoming Allies

Aims

- To define the concept of being an ally

- To relate being an ally to breaking the cycle of violence

- To begin a commitment from each student to become an ally

Skills

Students will

- Define what being an ally means

- Describe the qualities of a good ally

- Identify practical ways to be an ally

- Raise their expectations of alliance from other students

Preparation

- You will need the Power Chart from the last session, butcher paper, and copies of Handouts 6, 7, and 8.

To Begin: Overview on Allies

Ask students to review out loud the meaning of *oppression* and *internalized oppression*. Then ask them what the word *ally* means to them.

We will use the word ally to mean someone who backs up others. Allies intervene when others are mistreated, and they correct any misinformation, jokes, lies, or stereotypes they hear about them. An ally also interrupts any mistreatment others try to do to themselves.

An ally is a peacemaker—someone who helps break the cycle of violence. Someone can be an ally to people in her or his own group, to people in other groups on their side of the chart, or to nonpower groups from the power side. Let's look at the Power Chart to see where an ally can intervene.

Being Allies to Ourselves

Refer to the nonpower side of the Power Chart.

As members of nonpower groups, we have been told that we are not as good as or not as important as people across the line, that we are to blame for our problems. What messages like this do young people get? What messages do women get? What about people whose first language is not English? Older people?

When you are told over and over that you are unimportant, you might start to feel hopeless. You might think, "What's the use?" You may give up. Or you might stop caring what happens, and start doing things that risk your life. This is how oppression leads to internalized oppression, which leads to acts of violence against oneself, or self-destructive violence—seeing and mistreating yourself the way people from the power group see and treat you.

In what kinds of high-risk or hopeless ways do young people sometimes act?

Being an ally starts here—with yourself. Taking care of ourselves and getting support from others is the first way we can be allies.

Pass out Handout 6, Being Allies to Ourselves. Allow students a few minutes to answer the questions, then do the following brainstorming activity as a class:

- Make a list of self-destructive actions (such as putting yourself down or overeating).

- Describe ways to take care of yourself and to get support (talking to friends, eating well, respecting your body).

- Talk about what gets difficult about taking care of yourself (despair, peer pressure, lack of money or time).

- Name one thing you will each do to take better care of yourself.

Being Allies to Others in Our Groups

Explain to students that, just as we are taught to disrespect ourselves and blame ourselves for our problems, we learn to disrespect others in our group. We see the same messages about them that we see about ourselves.

Given all the negative messages we receive, having faith and confidence in and respect for other people in our group is not easy. For example, what negative messages do students sometimes get from teachers? What do students learn from these messages about treating each other? How do women learn to separate themselves from and mistreat each other or put each other down? How do people of color get taught to separate themselves from and mistreat other people of color?

Being an ally to others in your group is not always easy because of all the pressure to compete against and blame each other. But to stop the violence, we must stop fighting each other. We must become allies.

Pass out Handout 7, Being Allies to Each Other. As before, allow several minutes for writing, then conduct this brainstorming activity as a class:

- Describe violence that occurs among young people.

- Describe ways to be allies for other young people in the school (such as respecting others, not putting others down, supporting others taking care of themselves, interrupting when others are pressured to do drugs or to engage in high-risk behavior).

- Think of one person you could be a better ally to and what it is that you can do.

Being Allies Across the Line

Finally, remind students that everyone is in groups on both sides of the Power Chart.

As we grow older, we get into more of the power groups. We accumulate power, at least in the adult category. As members of power groups, we are taught to put down and abuse those with less power—to take out our feelings of pain, violation, and anger on those less able to protect themselves. And then we are taught to blame them for the violence.

When people in a more powerful group become allies of those with less social, political, or economic power, they help break the cycle of violence. When adults are allies of young people—and men of women, white people of people of color, and teachers of students—the whole system of power and violence is challenged.

In each of the four alliances mentioned above, ask students what the people in the power group could do to be allies to people in the nonpower group.

Defining the Role of an Ally

Break the class into small groups to discuss the following questions:

- Pick a nonpower group from the Power Chart. Make a list of what you would expect most from a person in the corresponding power group who intended to be an ally to people of that nonpower group. How would an ally stop the oppression against members of the nonpower group? How would an ally interrupt internalized oppression?

- Make a list of what would not be helpful from that ally.

As a class, wrap up the activity by brainstorming a final list on a sheet of butcher paper. Entitle it "What a Real Ally Does."

Closure

Pass out Handout 8, The Ally Pledge. Ask students to take it home and think (and write) about whatever might get in the way of their keeping the pledge, and what they need to be able to sign it in good conscience.

Close with the following, and any thoughts or feelings the students want to share with the group:

Everything we do for the rest of this course will be about making us strong allies of each other. By becoming allies we take down the wall that separates the two sides of the Power Chart. Being allies to one another is also the way we heal from all the bruises—the violence—that's been done to our hearts.

Handout 6 _Being Allies to Ourselves_

List things you do, or you see others your age do, that are self-destructive or dangerous.

Describe things you could do to be a better ally to yourself. For example, what would make and keep you physically healthy? What would help you feel mentally healthy? What would help you be physically safe? What would help you grow mentally and physically?

What gets in the way of taking care of yourself? List things that other people are responsible for that get in the way; then list barriers that you put up.

Name one thing you will do to take better care of yourself physically, one thing you will do to take better care of yourself mentally, and one thing you will do to take better care of your "heart."

Write the name of a nonpower group you are a member of. Describe the kinds of violence that occur among members of your group.

Describe ways to be an ally to other young people that you know (such as respecting them, not putting them down, supporting them in taking care of themselves, or interrupting pressure on them to do drugs or to engage in high-risk behavior).

What gets difficult about being an ally (such as negative messages, competition, peer pressure, or harsh judgments)?

Think of one person you could be a better ally to. What are the first, second, and third actual things you can do to be a better ally to that person?

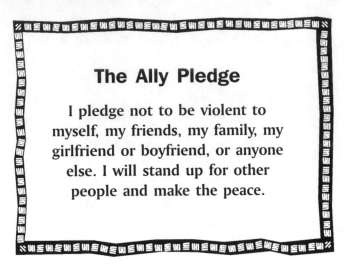

The Ally Pledge

I pledge not to be violent to myself, my friends, my family, my girlfriend or boyfriend, or anyone else. I will stand up for other people and make the peace.

An Ally I Know

Draw a picture of, tell a story about, or write a description of someone who is a strong ally.

How Violence Is Learned

Aims

- To introduce the concept of adultism and its role in violence

- To understand problems such as drug abuse, weapon use, eating disorders, and suicide as expressions of internalized adultism

- To understand violence among youth as a form of internalized adultism as well as a coping strategy

Skills

Students will

- Define *adultism* and identify examples of it

- Identify examples of internalized adultism

- Understand and identify examples of violence against peers and self-directed violence

- See other youth as allies in preventing all forms of violence

Preparation

- You will need the Power Chart and copies of Handout 9 and On Your Own sheet 4. You will also need a flipchart to record and save student comments.

- Review the "youth stand-up" categories and decide which categories to include and which to omit, based upon how safe it would be to use each category in class. (Alternatively, you might place difficult categories at the end of the stand-up and have students stay seated while you read them, to enable students simply to think about them.)

To Begin: Overview on Adultism

Refer to the "adult/youth" line on the Power Chart. In your own words, set the context for this session on adultism.

We make the assumption (as in the Heart Exercise) that we are not born violent. Neither are we born to accept violence. Something had to prepare us for the roles we find ourselves playing out in our violent society. Where does it start?

In the Heart Exercise, we saw that it starts with the bruises we received as children. Messages about being less powerful and being mistreated, or being more powerful and getting to mistreat others, were learned and practiced in childhood. By the time we are adults we have often learned to cope with a violent world by being violent, abusive, and self-destructive, or by being passive and unresponsive.

Young people are vulnerable and subjected to many kinds of violence from the adults and adult institutions around them. This type of violence is systematic: everyone either is or was a young person, and everyone goes through this basic training in power. We will call this systematic violence against young people adultism.

Pass out Handout 9, Adultism, and give students a few minutes to review it, or have volunteers read portions of the text out loud. As a class, discuss and clarify the ideas presented on the handout.

Adultism Visualization

Explain that you would now like students to participate in a nonverbal exercise designed to help them get in touch with how adultism makes them feel.

Have students get comfortable in their seats, close their eyes, go inside themselves, and listen as you read some or all of the following phrases in an appropriately "adult" tone of voice. Explain that some of the phrases may have been spoken to them directly; some they may have heard spoken to others. All they have to do is notice what they feel when they hear each phrase.

- "Not now. I don't have time."

- "You're too young to understand."

- "We'll talk about it later."

- "Go to your room!"

- "Not until you finish your homework."

- "Clean your plate."

- "I work my fingers to the bone for you."

- "Wait until *you* have children."

- "Wait until your father gets home."

- "When I was your age, I had it a *lot* harder."

- "Do what I say."

- "Not in *my* house you don't."

- "Because I said so."

- "Sit up. Sit up straight."

- "Don't you talk back to me."

- "Is that the best you can do?"

- "You're just a kid."

- "Pay attention when I'm talking to you!"

- "You're stupid."

- "Shut up."

- "You show me some respect."

- "This hurts me more than it hurts you."

- "Don't tell your mother about this; it's just our secret."

- "You get right upstairs and change into something decent."

- "Turn off that damn TV!"

- "Get the hell out of here!"

- "All right, *now* you're gonna get what's coming to you."

- "I brought you into this world—and I can take you out!"

Now, ask students to turn to a partner and take one minute each to talk about the *feelings* that came up as they heard the different phrases. Emphasize that feelings are often hard to talk about and that we may try to get intellectual about them instead. Point out that feelings are almost always just one word—like "angry," "furious," "humiliated"—or a series of single words.

Youth Stand-Up

Explain to students what a stand-up exercise is. You will read a category aloud, and students to whom the category applies will stand. Everyone in the class should notice who is standing and who isn't, and take note of their own feelings. Then you will ask students to sit down, and you will read the next category.

The purpose of this stand-up is to help us learn about some of the experiences of adultism that young people share. When they happen to you, you may feel all alone; it helps to know that lots of young people are going through some of the same experiences you are.

All you have to do during this exercise is notice how you feel. If you think a particular category applies to you but you don't want to stand up, you don't have to; you have a right to pass. If you choose to pass, please notice why you did, what it feels like to remain seated, and what it would take to make it safe for you to stand up for every category that applies to you.

Read the following items to the class. Allow ample time between each item for students to notice their own feelings and to notice who is standing and who is sitting.

Please stand up silently if

1. You have ever been called a name by an older person

2. Your dress or appearance was ever criticized by an adult

3. You have ever been called stupid or made to feel less intelligent by an adult

4. Adults have ever ignored you, served you last, or watched you suspiciously in a store

5. You have ever been told you were too young to understand

6. Your personal privacy was ever invaded in any way by an adult

7. You have ever been lied to by an adult

8. You have ever been cheated out of money by an adult

9. You were ever paid less than an adult for doing equal work

10. You were ever stopped by the police on the street

11. You were ever arrested or made part of the juvenile justice system

12. You have ever seen an adult you know acting under the influence of drugs or alcohol

13. An adult refused to hold you, hug you, or show you affection when you wanted it

14. You were ever left for a long period of time, or were left alone when you didn't want to be, or were ever abandoned by an adult

15. You have ever been physically restrained or trapped by an adult

16. You have ever been put on restriction by an adult

17. You were ever yelled at by an adult

18. An adult has ever physically threatened you

19. You have ever been held or touched by an adult in a way you didn't want to be held or touched

20. You have ever been hit or beaten by an adult

Reflection on the Visualization and Stand-Up

Have students take two minutes each to talk to a partner about feelings, observations, and questions that were raised by the exercise.

In a class discussion, encourage students to talk about whatever came up in the visualization or the stand-up or was shared in the pairs. Start by asking for feelings. As students name various feelings, ask for a show of hands to identify whether each feeling is shared by others.

Ask questions to help the class reflect on their experiences.

Were there any surprises? Did any stand-up questions or visualization phrases really stand out? What questions or phrases could have been added to the list? How do the visualization and the stand-up experiences relate to what you have learned about adultism?

To extend the discussion, you may want to ask these questions:

- Who are some people who have power over you?

- Who is one person your age or younger that you have some power over?

- Have you ever passed your frustration, anger, or pain on to that person or someone else less powerful than you?

- Have you ever felt so powerless, vulnerable, or hurt that you did something hurtful to yourself?

Closure

Express the following closing statement and check-out question in your own words.

Being young is not easy. You have a lot to learn in an increasingly complex and often dangerous world. We have talked a lot about ways that young people are vulnerable to violence from adults, but that does not change everything. When you leave class today, your school, your family, and your government will still be controlled by adults—people who will make decisions about your life, usually without you having much of a voice in those decisions.

You have figured out many ways of coping with this difficult reality. Some of those coping strategies will help make your life better; some will bring more problems into your life. What are some coping strategies that have worked for you? Do they still work? Which ones haven't worked so well?

Some of you are in difficult relationships with adults right now. You may be angry at them; you may be feeling abused by them; and you may want to go and talk to them or confront them. But you probably also know by now that those actions may not work, or that they may expose you to their anger or even to abuse.

One of our agreements is to "take care of yourself." To take care of yourself, talk to someone you can trust. Think about how you can safely bring these ideas up with adults. We will be spending more time, as we get further into this program, planning solid steps you can take to "make the peace."

As you leave today, I would like each of you to think of one specific way you can support another young person in being powerful against adultism without hurting themselves or others. What is one thing that you can do?

Pass out On Your Own sheet 4 and answer any questions about it. Remind students that they will need to bring their filled-out On Your Own sheet 2, My Family Tree, to the next session. Encourage students who haven't yet done so to finish their family trees and, if you will be designating a table for such items, to bring in photos and objects reflecting their family histories.

What if . . .

Some students deny that adultism exists?   Some students may remark that they haven't been mistreated by adults, or that their parents aren't like that, or that some adults may be bad but most are not. It is important to point out that we are speaking about oppression—*systematic* mistreatment. Some of us are fortunate to have nonabusive, supportive parents, but we are still vulnerable to violence, mistreatment, and discrimination from teachers, officials, neighbors, shopkeepers, employers, and other adults in positions of power.

Some students blame young people for what adults do to them?   Some students may claim that because kids are stupid, inexperienced, reckless, or naïve, they need adults to take charge and to tell them what to do. Remind these students that adult guidance and support—which every young person needs—are quite different from mistreatment. Setting limits is different from physical or verbal abuse. Internalized adultism leads us to think that young people need or deserve abusive treatment—which is why youth sometimes get blamed for the mistreatment that happens to them. We must remember that *adults are responsible for the injustices of adultism.* Violence, disrespect, discrimination, and harassment should play no part in childraising; there is no legitimate justification for them.

What it is

Adultism is the systematic exploitation, mistreatment, and abuse of young people by adults. (*Exploitation* means to take advantage of or to rob someone or a group of people of their labor, culture, energy, or possessions. *Mistreatment* means to treat unfairly or unjustly. *Abuse* is any form of violence—verbal, emotional, physical, or sexual.)

Who it affects

Everyone, particularly young people.

How it is enforced

Physical and sexual violence; neglect; police harassment; lack of trust and respect from adults; extreme pressure to succeed or harsh criticism of abilities; attacks on self-esteem; being paid less for equal work; lack of safe alternative living arrangements for youth in abusive families; adult stereotypes of young people.

How it might look at school

Lack of youth participation in decisions about curriculum, teaching methods, staffing, and how resources are distributed; arbitrary and unequal distribution of money and equipment to schools; tracking or separating students by ability or grade point average; inadequate funding for schools, youth recreation, and youth health; withholding of information and services from young people; blaming youth for violence, drugs, teenage sexuality, and bad schools.

How it is internalized

Violence against peers: Fights between guys and fights between girls; gossip and rumors; academic, athletic, and physical competition; put-downs and disrespect; gang violence; dating violence.

Self-destructive violence: Self-blame; apathy; hopelessness; drug use; suicide; eating disorders; high-risk activity and high-risk sexual activity; compulsive achievement; promiscuity; prostitution.

Who are allies

Adults can be allies to young people, and young people can be allies to each other.

How it has been resisted

Youth have led many of the struggles for freedom and democracy and the end of injustice including the civil rights movement in the United States, the anti-apartheid movement in South Africa, the Intifada in Palestine and Israel, and the movement for democracy in China and in several eastern European countries. Forms of resistance include protests, youth organizing, youth solidarity, passive and active resistance to adult authority, and innovative cultural forms such as music (rock and roll, rap), graffiti, and styles of dress.

List three ways you have seen youth cope with pressure by hurting others.

List three ways you have seen youth cope with pressure by hurting themselves in some way.

Describe one way you have seen young people break the cycle of violence in your school, their families, or the neighborhood by being powerful together or resisting violence without hurting others or themselves.

Race, Class, and Gender:
The Difference that Difference Makes

Sessions 6 and 7 zero in on the connections of violence to racial, regional, and cultural differences. Session 6 enables students to look at their own and each others' histories and the early messages they received about each other; Session 7 looks at racism and anti-Semitism, the violence associated with them, and first steps for students to become allies against this violence.

Session 8 explores another difficult issue that is intertwined with racism: economic class. The session discusses how differences in wealth, job opportunities, and status can lead to violence, and it helps youth build alliances to avoid violence based on economic differences.

Sessions 9 and 10 look at male and female relations. Session 9 focuses on gender-role training and the role that heterosexism and homophobia play in producing violence. Session 10 focuses on sexual harassment and how males can be allies to females and females to each other.

The flow of the lessons will vary considerably based on who is in your class and the cultural makeup of your school and the surrounding community. At particular points, alternative exercises are presented, keyed to the racial and gender composition of your class. Consult the sections on gender, race, and economic class issues in the Introduction (see pages 18–22) for further suggestions.

Who I Am, Where I'm From

Aims

■ To examine the concepts of race and culture and their role in violence

■ To develop respect for racial and cultural diversity

■ To build interracial communication

Skills

Students will

■ Identify and take pride in their own cultural identities

■ Learn about others' cultural identities

■ Define *race* and *culture*

Preparation

■ You will need the Power Chart and copies of On Your Own sheet 5. You will also need three prepared sheets of butcher or chart paper (see "Early Messages About Difference" on pages 79–80) and markers.

To Begin: Overview on Racial and Cultural Heritage

Take a few minutes for students to share what it was like for them after the session on adultism—what they noticed at school, in the neighborhood, or at home since the last session.

Introduce the topics for the next three sessions: race, culture, and economic class and their connection to violence.

Today's session will center on defining culture and race by looking at who we are and where we come from.

Students should have completed family trees (On Your Own sheet 2) with ethnic heritage, occupations, and geographical places noted for each generation. Encourage all students to display their ancestry artifacts and to look over what the other students have brought.

Working Definitions of Culture and Race

Refer to the whites/people of color and the Gentiles/Jews lines on the Power Chart. Acknowledge that the concepts of race and culture are understood differently by different people and thus are often confusing.

In this class we will use the word culture to describe all the different things that identify you and where you come from—like race, ethnicity, and what religion, if any, you practice. What are some other examples of culture?

List on the board all the words students suggest, which may include race, ethnicity, religion, country or nation, region or neighborhood, country or city, language spoken, age, financial status, and social class.

Culture means all of these things—all the ways people live together and define themselves. We each participate in family, community, school, geographic, linguistic, economic, and religious cultures based on who we are and who we associate with. Our "cultures" are what we inherit from our family and community—which we in turn modify and pass on to our descendants.

Write the following list on the board:

Racial/Cultural Identity

African-American

Arab-American

Asian-American

Native American/Indian

Pacific Islander

White/European-American

Christian

Jewish

Islamic

Buddhist

Multiheritage (several heritages, at least one of which is of color)

and many others

Because of thousands of years of migration and intermarriage—and outright violence like conquest and rape—people are not biologically distinct from each other except in superficial characteristics such as eye color, hair color, skin color, and facial features. Even in these areas, it is hard to make any generalizations about social or cultural differences based on physical differences.

Unfortunately, this has not kept people from using such differences to justify unequal treatment of and injustice toward others.

In fact, even the groups listed here are really combinations of cultures. A person isn't just Indian, but comes from a nation or nations such as Cheyenne, Iroquois, Cherokee, and Pomo; a person isn't just Jewish, but Sephardic Jewish, for example; or just Christian, but Lutheran; or just Moslem, but Shi'ite; or just European, but Italian.

Take a minute to talk about the designation *multiheritage*. Note that in many ways every person has multiple heritages; if that multiheritage includes ancestry, for example, from people of color or Jewish, Buddhist, or Islamic people, it can expose people to social mistreatment.

Students may want to acknowledge specific European ancestry such as Italian, Greek, or Irish. List these in connection with the European-American category, keeping examples focused on how people are seen and classified "on the street" in the United States.

Now that students have working definitions of *race* and *culture*, establish the connection between these concepts and violence.

Racism and anti-Semitism are systems of exploitation of people that use superficial physical, cultural, religious, or heritage differences between people to justify inequality and violence. The injustice of racism, the exploitation of people of color, damages the lives of people of color and white people alike. We discuss anti-Semitism as the foremost example of continuous religious/ cultural exploitation found in Western society, affecting both Jews and non-Jews. Of course Islamic peoples and other religious/cultural groups also experience full-scale exploitation, but anti-Semitism, like racism, has been alive in Western society for over 2500 years. We can't make the peace where racism and anti-Semitism exist.

Exploitation is when one group of people takes advantage of a power imbalance to rob—"rip off"—the land, money, labor, artifacts, culture, and traditions of another group.

Cultural Introductions

Divide the class into groups of four by inviting students to pair up with someone they don't know very well and then asking partners to pair up.

Explain that in their group, each person will have two minutes to do the following:

1. State their full name

2. Define their culture—say as much as they know about their racial or ethnic, religious or nonreligious, and regional background

3. Mention someone of their ancestry they look up to and why

4. If applicable, share anything new they found out in doing the family tree

Encourage participants not to identify themselves as just a mixture—as a "mutt" or a "Heinz 57"—but to relate as much about their heritage as they know. Anything at all they can say about their culture is acceptable. If individuals did not fill out the family tree, ask them to explain why in one or two sentences. Write the four steps given above on the board or use a transparency for easy student reference.

As an example, briefly respond to each step yourself. State your full name, talk about your cultural background, and mention someone from your ancestry, alive or not, personally related to you or not, famous or not, whom you look up to, and explain why.

Time the exercise, rotating presenters at two-minute intervals. If time allows, invite students to share how it felt to do the exercise.

Early Messages About Differences

Refer to the "Racial/Cultural Identity" chart that you created on the board.

People are often treated unequally based upon where they are from and who they are. Some of this treatment reflects the ways people came to be part of the United States and the places they occupy in society. In the next two sessions we will look at the oppression that separates people along these lines—how it affects us at this school, and what we can do about it.

One of the ways oppression works to separate us from each other is by teaching us lies about the people in these groups.

Separate the class into three groups. Give each group one of the following statements, written on butcher paper, to consider.

Group 1: Think of the earliest messages of any kind that you received that people of color were different from, or less valuable than, white people. State what happened and how it felt to get this "information."

Group 2: Think of the earliest messages of any kind that you received that Jewish people were different from, or less valuable than, Christians. State what happened and how it felt to get this "information."

Group 3: Think of the earliest messages of any kind that you received that immigrants, refugees, or non-English speakers were different from, or less valuable than, English-speaking people in the United States. State what happened and how it felt to get this "information."

Explain that students are to think of a personal experience of witnessing, or being told, that the members of the less powerful group identified were somehow less than people in the corresponding more powerful group.

Appoint two cofacilitators—female and male, if possible—for each group. Ask them to have all their group members, in silence, remember such experiences; then have several group members share their experiences and the associated feelings; and then have the entire group list the negative messages they heard and how they were affected by them.

Closure

After the class reconvenes, have a few students report what new insights they acquired from today's discussion and exercises.

Distribute On Your Own sheet 5, Who Came Here When? Explain that this will help us look at our origins in this country and what effect how we got here has on who we are today.

What if . . .

Some white or Christian students lack a strong sense of their cultural or ethnic background?   The parents, grandparents, or great-grandparents of some students may have at one time clearly identified with a particular cultural background. It is usually fairly easy to redirect these students to this cultural heritage, even if they deny its importance or value. The families of some white students may have assimilated over several generations, or have such a mixture of European heritages that they truly cannot reconstruct an ethnic identity. These students can still usefully reflect on the white Christian culture of which they are a part.

Some students say they are "simply American" and have no other culture?   Point out that everyone, except perhaps Native Americans, came to this country and brought with them unique customs, traditions, foods, and celebrations. What is "American" today is a mixture of many cultures. That process continues as new immigrants bring their cultures to add to American life. The important question is, "Who are *you* and how did you get here?"

Some students question what this process has to do with them?   Students may make such comments as, "This is all ancient history," or "Isn't the point to find our similarities, not focus on our differences?" or "Things have changed—it isn't like that anymore." While many things have changed over the years, racism and anti-Semitism remain, and there is significant injustice in our country based on cultural differences. You can point to many examples, from the uprisings in Los Angeles to job and housing discrimination, to segregated schools and hate crimes. If possible, offer local examples as well.

Some students hold extreme white supremacist or anti-Semitic opinions?   Some students have been raised in families where they are taught such views. It is important to allow these students to state their opinions without letting them dominate the discussion. Remind these students that we are here to talk about reducing violence and making the peace. Whether you like a person or a group of people or not, *everyone* deserves to be safe—no one deserves to be attacked for who they are.

Here is a list of different categories of people who came to live in the United States.

Native Americans

Refugees

Migrant Workers

Slaves

Servants

Immigrants (for this exercise, this means immigrants who did not come to the United States as slaves, servants, or migrant workers)

Colonized peoples (this means people who were annexed to the United States by colonial action, such as people from the Southwest, Puerto Rico, Cuba, and the Philippines)

Write about the following questions.

1. What people—including ethnicity, race, and class or economic group—fit in each category?

2. Except for Native Americans, how did each category of people get here?

3. How was each category of people treated?

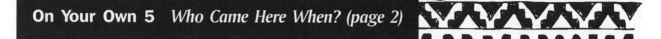

4. How might you have felt about how you became part of the process of forming the United States if you had been a member of each category?

5. How did—and does—each category of people experience violence?

6. How are the descendants of each category still affected by violence?

7. Locate your ancestors on the list. How does it feel to be a member or descendant of that category of people?

Who We're Going to Be

Aims

■ To build an understanding of racism and anti-Semitism and their effects on young people

■ To build cross-racial alliance

■ To teach cooperation and support through alliance

Skills

Students will

■ Define and describe *racism* and *anti-Semitism*

■ Identify the effects of racism and anti-Semitism on young people

■ Identify the effects of racism on people of color, immigrants, people of multiple heritages, and white people

■ Identify first steps for intervening in and preventing racism and anti-Semitism at their school

Preparation

■ Review the racism and anti-Semitism stand-up exercises on pages 86–94. Decide which of the three exercises you will use in this session and how you will conduct it.

■ You will need the Ally Pledge, copies of Handouts 10 and 11, and On Your Own sheet 6.

To Begin: Overview on Racism and Anti-Semitism

Remind students of the Agreements and review what has happened in the last two sessions, including the discussions about early messages young people receive about race. Ask whether students have any new thoughts or experiences to share. Acknowledge, without trying to answer or persuade, any difficulties with or objections to the discussions about race so far.

Definitions of Racism and Anti-Semitism

Pass out Handout 10, Racism, and Handout 11, Anti-Semitism. Answer any questions students have about them. On the board, write the following categories which represent the majority of people in the United States who face racial and religious exploitation. Explain that most of the Jewish people in the United States are of European origin, and for the purposes of the exercises on racism may be considered white, but they still encounter anti-Semitic violence and discrimination. Most Jewish people elsewhere in the world are people of color, and face both racism and anti-Semitism.

African/Afro-Caribbean

Arab/Middle Eastern

Asian/South Asian/Southeast Asian

Latino/Chicano/Hispanic/Puerto Rican/Cuban

Native American/Indian

Pacific Islander

Jewish

Brainstorm with the class about specific forms of violence ("anything that denies human integrity, and leads to hopelessness and helplessness") that happen to each group. Include both individual incidents and institutional discrimination in the areas of jobs; housing; neighborhood and community; law enforcement; education; media representation; historical and political representation; and wealth. Highlight any recent or contemporary examples.

If students can't think of examples for a particular group, offer some of your own and ask questions such as:

- Why might we not know about the real experiences of people in this group?

- Where do we normally get information about people in this group?

- How much real information do these sources provide us about people in this group?

- If you think that the information may not be trustworthy, can you say why that is so?

Explain that an important source of and consequence of inequality and discrimination is exclusion from certain parts of society. For example, how are people of color and Jewish people sometimes excluded from neighborhoods, high political offices, and corporate management? How are these people then blamed for the violence and exclusion that happens to them? Encourage students to be as specific as possible for each group.

Finally, lead a discussion of whether it is possible to make the peace when racial injustice and inequality exist. What if the students made peace in this school, but there was still violence in the rest of the city?

Racism and Anti-Semitism Exercises

What you do next will depend on whether the class is predominantly white (in that case, conduct the White Stand-Up), predominantly students of color (do the People of Color Stand-Up), or more or less evenly divided between youth of color and whites (do the Students of Color Speak-Out).

White Stand-Up

Conduct a version of the White Stand-Up exercise with 12 to 15 categories or questions that you have selected in advance from the following list, or hand out the full list of the stand-up categories for students to review silently. First, introduce this exercise by talking about white people's experience of racism and anti-Semitism.

What does all this mean for white people—people with European backgrounds?

Racism also operates to deny the different ethnic heritages of white people, persuading whites to believe that they have no cultural heritage but are instead a bland monoculture. It falsifies their view of the world, and it saddles them with resentfulness, unawareness, fear, guilt, or hate when the subject of racism arises. White people's early messages and experiences of learning about racism and anti-Semitism are hurtful, often coming from people they trusted or loved who were passing on their own hurt. All of these effects are happening to white children right now.

The exercise we are going to do can help demonstrate just how that training takes place, and what the costs are for whites.

Read aloud each category that you have selected, and ask white, non-Jewish students to stand silently whenever a statement applies to them, notice who's standing with them, and notice how they feel. Then they sit, and the next statement is read. All have the right to pass, but are asked to notice their feelings if they do so. If white Jewish students are present, acknowledge that categories may apply to them as white people, but ask them to remain seated and notice how it feels to watch the stand-up as white *and* Jewish young people.

Please stand up silently if

1. You don't know exactly what your European/American heritage is, your great-grandparents' names are, or what regions or cities your ancestors are from.

2. You have ever been told or believe you have a "Heinz 57" or "mutt" heritage.

3. You grew up in a household where you heard derogatory racial terms or racial jokes.

4. You grew up in a household where you heard that racism was bad and that you were never to notice out loud, comment, or remark upon racial differences (for example, people told you, "It doesn't matter if you're purple or green, we're all equal; you shouldn't notice a person's color").

5. You grew up in a household where you heard that racism was bad, and that some or all white people were racist and you would always have to fight it.

6. You grew up in a household where you heard derogatory comments about Jewish people.

7. You grew up, lived, or live in a neighborhood, or went to school or a camp, that as far as you knew was exclusively white.

8. You grew up, lived, or live in a neighborhood, or went to school or a camp, that as far as you knew was exclusively Christian.

9. You grew up with people of color who were servants, maids, gardeners, or babysitters in your house.

10. You did not meet people of color in person, or socially, before you were well into your teens.

11. You did not meet Jewish people in person, or socially, before you were well into your teens.

For the next category, after you stand, remain standing if the next item also applies to you.

12. You were ever given pictures or images—in magazines, on film, on radio, on television, or in songs—of

   ■ Mexicans depicted as drunk, lazy, or illiterate

   ■ Asians depicted as exotic, cruel, or mysterious

   ■ People from India depicted as excitable or silly

   ■ Arabs depicted as swarthy, fanatical, or crazed

- Blacks depicted as violent or criminal

- Jews depicted as greedy, rich, or immoral

- Pacific Islanders depicted as fun-loving or lazy

- American Indians depicted as drunk, savage, or noble

- character roles from nonwhite cultures being acted by white actors

13. You were ever told not to play with a child or children of a particular ethnicity.

14. You were ever told not to notice or say anything about the ethnicity, race, or skin color of people of color.

15. You have ever felt that white culture is bland, empty, or boring; or that another racial group has more rhythm, athletic ability, or musical or artistic creativity; or that certain groups are better with their hands, better at math and technology, or better with money.

16. You have ever felt that people of another racial group are more spiritual than white people.

17. You have ever been attracted to a person from another racial group or to a Jewish person because it seemed exotic, exciting, or challenging.

18. You have ever witnessed people of color being mistreated in any way by white people.

19. You were ever taught to be afraid of or to distrust Jewish people or people of color.

20. You have ever felt nervous or fearful or have stiffened up when encountering people of color in a neutral public situation (for example, in an elevator or on the street).

21. You have ever worked in a place where all the people of color who were employees had more menial jobs than yours and other white employees'.

22. You have ever eaten in a public place where all the clientele were white, and the only people of color present were service workers.

23. You have ever been in or attended an organization, group, meeting, or event that people of color protested as racist or that you knew or suspected to be racist.

24. You have ever felt racial tension in a situation and were afraid to say anything about it.

25. You have ever had degrading jokes, comments, or put-downs about people of color or Jewish people made in your presence and felt powerless to protest them.

26. You have ever seen a person of color being put down or attacked verbally or physically and did not intervene.

27. You have ever felt guilty or powerless to do anything about racism.

28. You have ever felt embarrassed by, separate from, superior to, or more tolerant than other white people on the issues of racism or anti-Semitism.

29. You have ever felt embarrassed by, separate from, superior to, or more tolerant than other people in your immediate family on the issues of racism or anti-Semitism.

30. You have ever felt angry or frustrated or tired or weary of dealing with racism and hearing about racial matters.

31. You have ever had a close friendship or relationship with another white person that was damaged or lost because of a disagreement about racism.

32. You have ever had a close friendship or relationship with a person of color that was affected or endangered because of racism between the two of you or from others.

33. You have ever lost a friendship with a person of color that, when you think of it now, may have happened because of racism.

34. You do not currently have a close or significant friendship or relationship with a person of color.

Close the exercise by having white students talk in pairs or small groups about their feelings and thoughts during the exercise. If there are people of color or Jewish people in the class, have them meet to share their feelings about watching the stand-up.

Then, as a class, have students discuss this question: *How are white people hurt by racism?*

Steer the discussion toward how white people are hurt by racism—not how they are hurt by individual encounters with people of color, but how they are hurt by the systems of racial inequality in the United States. If there are a few people of color or Jewish people in the class, do not let the burden of describing or pointing out racism or anti-Semitism fall on their shoulders, nor expect them to pacify the white students' discomfort about discussing racism and anti-Semitism.

Display the Ally Pledge.

Part of making the peace is for white people to be allies to people of color and Jewish people in the struggle to end racism and anti-Semitism. What next steps can you take to be an ally to people of color and Jewish people?

Ask several students—or all, if time allows—to share their next step.

People of Color Stand-Up

Conduct this activity as above, as a condensed stand-up exercise, or as a handout reviewed silently. An alternative format is to start out with a couple of these categories and then ask people of color to take turns asking more "Please stand if you ever..." questions. A fourth alternative is simply to have students state at length how they are affected by racism.

Read each statement that you have selected, and ask students of color to rise whenever a statement applies to them.

Please stand up silently if

1. Your ancestors, because of their race or ethnicity, were (a) forced to come to this country; (b) forced to relocate from where they were living in this country, temporarily or permanently; or (c) restricted from living in certain areas.

2. You have ever heard or overheard people saying that you or your people should leave, go home, or go back where you came from.

3. In your family, as a child, you were the intermediary between your parents and store clerks or public officials (such as social workers or school officials) because of language or other differences.

4. You were ever called names or otherwise ridiculed by someone you didn't know because of your racial or ethnic identity.

5. You were ever ridiculed by a teacher, employer, or supervisor because of your racial or ethnic identity.

6. You have ever been told by a white person that you are different from other people of your racial or ethnic group.

7. You have ever been told that you don't act (black, Latino, Asian, Arab, Indian, etc.) enough.

8. You have ever been told that you are too sensitive about racial matters or are acting too (black, Latino, Asian, Arab, Indian, etc.).

9. You have ever received less than full respect, attention, or response from a doctor, police officer, court official, city official, or other professional because of your race or ethnicity.

10. You have ever seen your racial or ethnic group portrayed on television or film in a derogatory way.

11. You have ever tried to change your physical appearance (such as your hair or skin color), mannerisms, speech, or behavior to avoid being judged or ridiculed because of your racial or ethnic identity.

12. You have ever been told to learn to speak "correct" or "better" English.

13. You were ever discouraged or prevented from pursuing academic or work goals, or tracked into a lower or vocational level, because of your racial or ethnic identity.

14. You were ever mistrusted or accused of stealing, cheating, or lying because of your racial or ethnic identity.

15. You have ever picked up that someone was afraid of you because of your racial or ethnic identity.

16. You have ever been stopped by the police because of your racial or ethnic identity.

17. You have ever been refused employment because of your racial or ethnic identity.

18. You have ever been paid less, treated less fairly, or given harder work than a white person in a similar position because of your ethnic or racial identity.

19. Your religious or cultural holidays have ever been disregarded at your job or your school and, for example, classes or meetings or work time were scheduled during those periods.

20. You have ever been refused housing, discouraged from applying for housing, or had to leave housing because of racial discrimination.

21. You have ever felt conspicuous, uncomfortable, or alone in a group of people because you were the only representative of your racial group.

22. You have ever felt uncomfortable or angry about a remark or joke made about your race or ethnicity but didn't feel safe to confront it.

23. You have ever felt the threat of violence because of your racial or ethnic identity.

24. You or close friends or family have ever been victims of violence because of your racial or ethnic identity.

25. You have ever been told by a white person that you are too sensitive, emotional, or angry when talking about racism.

Close the exercise by having students of color talk in pairs or small groups about their feelings and thoughts during the exercise. If there are white students in the class, have them meet to share their feelings about watching the stand-up.

Then, as a class, discuss the following questions.

- How does racism—discrimination and violence against people of color—lead people of color to direct violence at each other or at themselves?

- Who benefits when people of color commit violence against each other or against themselves?

- As people of color, what do you need to do to take care of each other and to fight racism in our school?

Encourage students to be as specific as possible about ways to interrupt the effects of internalized racism—violence directed at each other.

Display the Ally Pledge.

Making the Peace

Part of making the peace is for people of color to be allies to each other in the struggle to end racism and anti-Semitism. What next step can you take to be a better ally to other people of color?

Ask several students—or all, if time allows—to share their next step.

People of Color Speak-Out

The primary goal in a racially mixed class is to facilitate students talking to each other honestly and respectfully about racism and anti-Semitism, and to create enough safety so that students of color can "speak out" to white students and so that Jewish students can also be acknowledged. In schools where there are predominantly students of color but in which two or more racial groups have been in conflict (for example, African-American and recent Asian immigrants, Latinos and African-Americans, or Chinese and Koreans), conduct the Modified People of Color Speak-Out that follows (see pages 93–94).

If you have the time, consider preceding this exercise by having white students and students of color meet in separate groups and experience a shortened version of the Whites Stand-Up and People of Color Stand-Up respectively.

To conduct the Students of Color Speak-Out, have the students of color stand together in the front of the class. Tell the white students that this is an opportunity for them to hear directly what impact racism has on people of color. Ask them to listen quietly and attentively and to hold any feelings, comments, or responses until later. If you are white, these guidelines apply to you as well.

Read each of the following questions, and ask the students of color to speak out for a couple of minutes on each question. Encourage them to take their time, to decide among themselves what order to speak in, and to allow everyone in their group to participate.

1. What is one word, phrase, name, or statement that you never want to hear again about your racial or ethnic group?

2. What is one example of how racism affects you, your friends, or your family?

3. What is one way that you have seen racism happen in this school? (By "school," we mean the administration, staff, teachers, and neighbors as well as the students themselves.)

4. What do you need from white allies to stop racism?

After the group has finished their discussion of the last question, have the white students respond by stating what they learned from the speak-out and how it felt to listen to their classmates speak out to them.

Jewish People Speak-Out

If there are Jewish students in the class, repeat this exercise with them speaking out to the non-Jews. (In the speak-out questions above, substitute "anti-Semitism" for "racism" and "non-Jewish allies" for "white allies.")

Modified People of Color Speak-Out

For schools where there are predominantly students of color, or in which two or more racial groups have been in conflict, or in which Jews and students of color are the dominant groups, use the following modified version of the speak-out to help them become better allies to each other.

Have students of the different groups meet separately, if there is time, and then take turns as groups speaking out to each other. Invite students who have multiple heritages to choose which group it makes sense for them to be with—which one they are most often categorized as belonging to. If several students identify themselves as multi-heritage, have them meet in their own group.

Have each group stand before the class and take time to answer the questions; after each group speaks, the rest of the class repeats back to them what they heard. The groups answer questions 1, 2, and 3 as in the People of Color Speak-Out, then question 4 below:

4. What do you need from allies of the other groups here to stop racism (or anti-Semitism)?

Close with a class discussion about how white students, students of color, and Jewish students can work together in the school to stop racism. Where does it get hard to work together? Encourage each student to think about what specifically he or she can do to stop racial violence, discrimination, or inequality at the school. Ask white students how they can be better allies to people of color. Ask students of color how they can be better allies to each other.

Closure

Bring the class back together. Encourage students to continue talking—with each other, with friends, and with their families—about the issues and feelings that have come up in the classroom.

Discussing racism and anti-Semitism brings up complex and uncomfortable feelings for all of us. Our focus here is on stopping the violence—and to do that effectively, we must be honest about the violence that goes on in our community. That violence affects us all.

Pass out On Your Own sheet 6, My Economic History, and answer any questions about it. This exercise will prepare students to discuss economic issues as they affect them and cause violence in their lives.

Some white students deny the existence of racism or anti-Semitism? Students may make statements like "I treat everyone equally," or "In this country, everyone has an equal chance and it's their own fault if they don't succeed." Explain that one of the ways powerful groups keep their power is to deny that inequality exists. When it is impossible to deny the inequality any longer, powerful groups blame the group who is denied power. Point out ways that white students may have been taught to blame people of color or Jewish people. You can acknowledge that individual effort does make a difference in what we achieve in our lives while noting, at the same time, that our skin color and religion influence what opportunities are available to us and what kinds of obstacles we may or may not face.

Some students deny responsibility for anti-Semitism? If some students claim that this is a Christian country and that's just the way it is, point out that America was founded on the principle of separation of church and state, and that millions of Americans are Jewish, Buddhist, Moslem, or atheist. Some students may say that Jews are powerful and control everything, effectively blaming Jewish people for anti-Semitism. Keep the focus on institutional power—the corporate, political, and social leaders of this country—to point out that it is white Christians, not Jews, who make most of the decisions that affect our lives. Be careful not to blame the students; they are simply repeating misinformation they have received about Jews. You may want to help them locate resources for further information, including those listed on pages 173–176.

What it is

Racism is the exploitation, mistreatment, and abuse of one group of people by another based upon race. In the United States, this usually refers to exploitation of people of color by white people.

Who it affects

Everyone, particularly people of color.

How it is enforced

Job, educational, and housing discrimination; police brutality; unequal pay for equal work; lack of adequate health care; unequal funding for education; physical and sexual assault; negative stereotypes and lack of positive images on television and film; lack of representation in social, political, economic, and legal institutions.

How it might look at school

Lack of people of color in leadership at the administrative, teacher, or student levels; segregation of people of color into schools, programs, or classes with fewer resources, less status, or poorer future opportunities; tracking or separating students based on "ability"; denial that racism exists; lack of positive role models and images in the history, science, and literature curriculums; teasing, harassment, and stereotypes in student culture.

How it is internalized

Violence against peers: Interracial violence; gang- and drug-related violence; competition; put-downs, gossip, and rumors about other people of color; violence against women of color; denial that racism exists.

Self-destructive violence: Despair; self-blame; apathy; drug use; suicide; high-risk activity; undermining one's efforts to achieve; not taking oneself seriously; not taking care of oneself.

Who are allies

Every white person can be an ally to people of color. People of color can be allies to each other.

How it has been resisted

Liberation movements throughout the world have been led by people of color, including the Native American struggle for land and sovereignty; farmworker organizing; the civil rights movement; and women's, student, health care, and economic justice movements. People of color have created a rich legacy of resistance through music, dance, poetry, literature, art, and other forms of protest and direct action.

What it is

Anti-Semitism is prejudice, discrimination, and violence directed against people who are Jewish.

Who it affects

Everyone, particularly people who are Jewish.

How it is enforced

Housing and job discrimination; hate crimes; quotas; stereotypes and jokes; scapegoating for social problems; denial that anti-Semitism exists; denial of the Holocaust.

How it might look at school

Stereotypes and jokes about Jews; scapegoating for social problems; exclusion from clubs or social events; assumptions that everyone is Christian, shown by the celebration of Christian holidays in school and having school scheduled on Jewish holidays; Christian prayers or rituals at public events; invisibility of Jews and Jewish concerns.

How it is internalized

Violence against peers: Competition; put-downs; gossip and rumors about Jews; violence against Jewish women; denial that anti-Semitism exists.

Self-destructive violence: Despair; self-blame; apathy; drug use; suicide; denial; trying to change one's appearance; fear of being loud, pushy, aggressive, or even just visible as Jews; attempts to pass as Christian; undermining one's efforts to achieve; not taking oneself seriously; not taking care of one-self; holding impossible-to-reach standards for oneself.

Who are allies

Christians and other Gentiles (non-Jews) can be allies to Jewish people. Jews can be allies to each other.

How it has been resisted

Jewish people have participated in and been leaders in many struggles for social justice, fought against anti-Semitism in the United States, and fought to defend themselves against the Nazis during the Holocaust. Jews have fought for visibility as Jews and challenged individual acts of discrimination and violence.

Describe in detail what you know about your economic background by answering the following questions. If you are not comfortable writing your answers, answer the question in your mind. If you don't know some of the answers, ask family members who do.

1. What do your parents or the people who are raising you do for a living, paid or unpaid? Would you say their work is skilled or unskilled? Does it include manual or physical labor, or not? Do they supervise others, or not?

2. What level of formal education did your parents or the people who are raising you complete (for example, high school, some college education, or graduated from college)?

3. Where does the income that supports your family come from (for example, salary, wages, stocks and bonds, renters or roommates, social security or veteran payments, or public assistance)?

4. How many people live in your house now?

5. Where do you live (for example, in your own house, a rented house, public housing, an apartment, a trailer, a residential program, a shelter)?

6. How much private, personal space do you have where you live (for example, your own bedroom, a shared bedroom, a room with other family uses during the day, group sleeping quarters, transient)?

7. Where do you get most of your clothes (for example, made at home, hand-me-downs, used clothing store, discount store, department store, specialty store)?

8. Where does your family usually get food (for example, fast-food restaurant, convenience store, warehouse discount store, supermarket, grow or produce your own food, specialty market, sit-down restaurant)?

9. Do you earn money or otherwise bring income into your home? Is this income necessary to support others in your home? Is it necessary, or partly necessary, to support you?

10. What do you consider your economic background to be now? Note any way you think your economic or social standing might be different from that of your parent or parents and grandparents, or might have changed in the last few years in any direction, and why.

11. Is any of this difficult or uncomfortable for you to write about? Write about your feelings answering these questions and why you think you might feel this way.

12. Think of an incident at school in which you were made to think about your economic or class background—something somebody said or did that made you think about your family and money or social standing, whether positive or negative. Describe the incident, and write about how you felt.

Economic Class

Aims

- To introduce the concepts of social class, wealth, and poverty and explore their role in violence

- To build awareness of economic class

- To build respect for different economic backgrounds

- To build interclass communication

Skills

Students will

- Define *class* and *class-based violence*

- Identify effects of class-based violence among young people

- Identify and take pride in their own class identities

- Begin building cross-class alliances

Preparation

- Draw the Class Pyramid (see page 101) on chart paper, on a transparency, or on the board.

- Have the Power Chart on the board for easy reference. Students should have their homework for reference. You will need copies of Handout 12.

To Begin: Overview

Take a few minutes to allow students to talk about feelings and thoughts that came up when they profiled their economic background in the On Your Own 6 assignment. Acknowledge any difficulties, confusion, or feelings of embarrassment that this topic raises. Then, referring to the Rich/Poor line on the Power Chart, introduce this session's topic.

Today we will look at how violence is related to class—to how much money people have or don't have, where they get it, how they spend it, and what this means for young people.

Working Definition of Class

Have students volunteer examples and definitions of what the word *class* means, both economically and socially. Take several minutes to make sure that income, profession, status, and other markers of class are mentioned.

Draw the Class Pyramid[*] shown below on the board, on chart paper, or on a transparency, and display it in proximity to the Power Chart.

The Class Pyramid

Rich / Owners
1% of the population
Holds 48% of U.S. wealth
Independently wealthy
Over $3,000,000/household net worth
Average income over $400,000/year

Middle / Professional / Managerial
19% of the population — Holds 46% of U.S. wealth
Over $500,000/household net worth
Work for owners — Average income over $100,000/year

Poor / Front-line workers / Unemployed / Welfare / Homeless
80% of the population — Holds 6% of U.S. wealth
$38,000/household net worth — Average income $23,000/year

Review the pyramid for several minutes, discussing the details. Explain that the income figures are averages, and can vary in different regions.

You may point out that the top (rich) and bottom (poor) categories are taken directly from the Power Chart and that a new category has been added between them, one that is less powerful than the rich but more powerful than the poor.

One way that class works is to separate us from each other and put us in different categories—some toward the top, and some toward the bottom.

---

[*] Sklar, Holly. *Chaos or Community: Seeking Solutions, Not Scapegoats for Bad Economics.* Boston: South End Press, 1995.

Encourage a discussion of the information in the Class Pyramid by asking these questions:

■ What do "top" and "bottom" mean on this pyramid?

■ For each of the three categories, ask: Who is in this slot? What kind of work do they do? What are their neighborhoods like? How do they survive? How might they feel about the slot they are in?

■ For each of the three categories, ask: How is this slot different from the other two? How does being in this slot affect people?

Make sure students thoughtfully address the last question for each slot. You may notice some uncertainty about what it might be like for the "middle slot" people. If so, guide the discussion by having students focus upon how "middle" people feel about and are treated in relation to "rich" people, and how they feel about and are supposed to relate to "poor" people.

Classism and Violence

Review Martin Luther King Jr.'s definition of violence: "Anything that denies human integrity, and leads to hopelessness and helplessness." Promote a discussion of the connection between classism and violence by asking the following questions:

■ What kinds of violence happen to poor, working-class, and middle-class people from the rich, taking into account not only individual, social, political, and financial violence, but also "denial of integrity"?

■ What kinds of violence happen from the bottom of the Class Pyramid to the top?

■ What differences, if any, do you notice between the top-down violence and the bottom-up violence?

■ What kinds of violence, if any, happen *among* people who are poor or working class?

We call this system of violence classism: the daily, routine, institutional mistreatment of people based on their economic background. The people on the bottom of the Class Pyramid are targeted for violence; the people in the middle are both targeted and targeters; the people on the top are raised to be in positions of power. Poor and working-class people internalize classism when they attack each other; try to separate from one another; or put themselves down for not having enough money, education, or success.

Place students in groups of two or three for a few minutes to talk about what they have just heard and discussed and what they think about the economic pyramid. When the class reassembles, take some time for questions, reflections, and challenges. Acknowledge that this model is too simple to accurately portray all the complexities of class divisions—and that even just talking about class divisions can bring up many unsettling feelings.

As a final question, ask how this system of economic stratification benefits people at each level and what it costs them.

Class and Young People

Explain how the wealth in this country—and much of the world—is passed from generation to generation.

Children in rich families inherit money and land; go to good schools; have lots of learning opportunities through family travel, books, classes, and field trips, and have connections for getting into the best colleges and careers. Middle-class parents usually pass on educational opportunities and some money and connections to their children. Poor and working-class families have little wealth to pass on to their children.

Although Americans talk a great deal about this being a land of opportunity and that anyone can make it here, the reality is that a majority of young Americans will end up in the same financial situation as their parents.

Young people as a group have a special relationship to the Class Pyramid: you are being trained to take over your parents' position in the pyramid. Each of you has come from a place in the pyramid related to your family's wealth, and each of you spends time thinking about your economic future— what you are going to do, and how you are going to get by.

Stimulate a discussion about young people and economic class by asking the following questions:

- What kinds of things are happening in young people's lives that send them toward the bottom of the pyramid? Toward the middle? Toward the top?

- What might make it hard for you, if you wanted to, to move up from the slot your family is in? Besides hard work, what resources would it take? What would you gain? What would you have to give up?

- Many people say that if you work hard, you will be rewarded with financial success. Is this always true?

Divide the class into small groups, and have each group write a short list of responses to each of the four questions on Handout 12. Continue to display the Class Pyramid for students to refer to during this short exercise.

Closure: Building Class Alliances

Close the session by having groups share their thoughts about question 4 in the handout. How have young people at this school successfully reached across class divisions?

1. Where do you think this school would fit on the Class Pyramid based on the average wealth of students' families? Which schools in which nearby areas do you think are richer or poorer than this one?

2. How do you see economic class affecting young people's relationships at this school? Does class affect the cliques that are formed? Where people hang out at lunchtime? Who goes to which parties? What kinds of jokes or put-downs are made?

3. What violence has happened in the last year at this school that is related to money or class—that is, to someone responding to the pressures of the Class Pyramid?

4. How have young people at this school reached across class divisions?

Women and Men Together

Aims

- To introduce the concepts of sexism and violence against women

- To identify the training in gender roles

- To highlight the roots of violence against women in male and female socialization

- To build cross-gender alliances to stop and prevent violence against women

- To build female/female, male/male, and male/female solidarity

Skills

Students will

- Describe how children are trained into gender roles

- Identify sexism and internalized sexism

- Define *heterosexism* and *homophobia* and the role they play in enforcing gender roles

- Identify the costs of sexism to women in general and how women personally have been hurt

- Commit to specific steps to challenging sexism

Preparation

- You will need copies of Handouts 13, 14, 15, and 16 and On Your Own sheets 7, 8, and 9. You will also need a flipchart, markers, and tape, or blank transparencies.

To Begin: Overview on Gender Roles

Prepare the class for the Father-Son Role Play.

So far we have looked at how violence affects us all, female or male. We have examined the systematic mistreatment of young people (adultism), and we have analyzed the differences that race and class make on our position in the cycle of violence.

Our gender—whether we are female or male—also makes a difference in how we are in the world, how we are treated, how we are trained. During the next two sessions, we will examine more closely the difference that gender makes in our lives.

We will begin with a role play that will demonstrate how boys are trained to be men—men who can end up being violent or abusive to others. Later we will look at how girls are trained to be women. We will also talk about how homophobia—the fear of gays, of being gay, or of being thought gay—contributes to the violence we experience as women or men.

Father-Son Role Play

You will play the father in this role play. (A female teacher should indicate that she will play a male.) Choose a male student to play your son. Prepare the student by explaining the scenario; get agreement from him if you are going to make physical contact with him during the role play (for example, shoving him back into the chair).

Tell the class that _____ is playing your ten-year-old son. Explain that he has just come home from school and is sitting in the living room watching TV. (Let the student pick the show.) His father then enters the room, brandishing a report card.

F: What the hell are you doing? Turn off that TV! And what the hell is this? *(shows report card)*

S: It's my report card.

F: Your report card! If you're so smart, why were you dumb enough to get a D in math?

S: I did the best I could.

F: A D is the best you could do? You're just dumb!

S: That's not fair. *(starts to get up)*

F: *(shoves him down)* Don't you talk back to me! You hear, boy?

S: *(starts to cry)*

F: Oh, you gonna cry now? Huh? *(shakes son, hits him with report card)* Why don't you grow up and act like a man! *(stomps out)*

S: *(freezes)*

Step out of your role, and ask the student who played the son: How are you feeling right now about yourself? How are you feeling about your father? About what just happened?

Then, turn to the class and ask: What's going on here? Why is this fight happening? Who is responsible? Is this really about grades?

One thing the father told his son is to "act like a man." Let's talk about that.

Act-Like-a-Man Box   Ask the class what the boy in the role play was feeling during the scene. Write the list of feelings in the center of the board, and draw a circle around it.

Have the young men in the room pretend for a moment that they are ten years old and that there is an adult man—their father, stepfather, coach—who is yelling at them, saying, "Act like a man!" Say this in an angry tone of voice to each of them. Then, step back from the role and ask: What are you learning you are supposed to do when someone says that to you?

Outside of the circle on the board, list the characteristics that students name. Be sure to include *be tough* and its equivalents, and *don't cry.* Draw a box around the entire list and label it "Act Like a Man."

(A note on the word *macho.* Someone will probably mention *macho* as a male characteristic. Suggest an English term instead, and take a minute to explain that *macho* is a Spanish/Mexican term—having to do with honor and taking care of one's family—that has been misused negatively in English to mean tough and insensitive, and then reapplied to Latino men as a stereotype. To avoid this form of racism, it's best not to use the term at all.)

We call this our Act-Like-a-Man Box. Part of the message for men is: when you get hurt, take it in, keep it in, don't ever tell anyone. Hang tough; go it alone. If boys have the kinds of feelings that we see in the center of the box, and are trying to act the way we see on the outside—be tough, take the pain, don't show feelings except anger—how will they be when they grow up?

Continue with the development of the image on the board.

What names do boys or men get called if they try to step out of this box? (Write the names along the right side of box.) What is the purpose of these names? What are you supposed to do when someone calls you these names? These names are little slaps in the face, telling us to get back in the box. They're emotionally violent; they hurt us and make us want to change our behavior so we never get called these names again.

What happens to boys physically? How do they get treated physically to

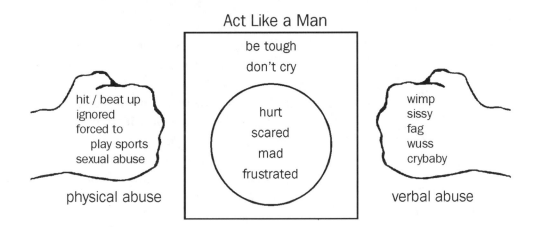

make sure they act like men? Write the list on other side of box. Then, en-close both lists with fists, and title the fists "verbal abuse" and "physical abuse."

Another kind of physical mistreatment that happens to boys is that one out of six boys is sexually abused before the age of 18. These boys are usually abused by a man who is not gay, who may seem like "everyone else"—he may have a wife and kids. What about the Act-Like-a-Man Box will make it real hard for a guy who's been sexually abused to talk about it and get help? What names will he be afraid he will be called? (Add students' suggestions to the "verbal abuse" fist.)

Part of the message this box gives men is this: when you get hurt, keep it in, don't ever tell anyone. When you raise a boy from the time he is a baby to take the pain, to keep it to himself, to show angry feelings and no others, you are training someone to walk around like a time bomb. What will happen when this man is 17 or 18 or 20 and finds himself getting angry about something?

Pass out Handout 13. Instruct students to fill in the box and the fists, adding any words that they want to. Ask them to notice in the next few days how men act and then add other words to the handout.

Allow students to talk about any thoughts that come up for them. Point out that we can see from the box that boys are not *born* violent; they continually get emotionally and physically "punched" to pressure them to stay in control. No boy wants it to be this way, and they all try to figure out how to deal with it in their own way.

Homophobia and Heterosexism

Point out any words in the "verbal abuse" list that refer to gays or imply homosexuality.

What is the purpose of these names? When boys hear them, what are they being taught about being close to other boys or men? What are they being told about gay men? How does this fear of being labeled keep men in the box?

Distribute Handout 14 and give students a few minutes to review it. In your own words, communicate these ideas:

Many of the words we use against boys—and against girls—have to do with being gay. Fag, sissy, wimp—these are fighting words for boys. Even the slightest hint that we are gay means we must change our behavior to prove we are in the box. The primary way we prove we aren't gay is to hurt or abuse someone else—we think that's the sign of being a real man. Homophobia—the fear of homosexuals, and the fear of being gay or of being thought gay—makes it unsafe for everyone.

Explain that homophobia contributes to the violence that lesbian, gay, bisexual, and sexually questioning youth experience. It makes them targets of violence, and it leads to internalized blame—which in turn can lead to self-destructive actions such as taking drugs or committing suicide. Homophobia is used against every young person who tries to get out of the box.

For example, if a boy plays the piano, likes dancing, gets good grades, is not interested in girls, is not good in sports, or simply annoys someone, he can be put down, abused, and pressured to change his behavior to prove he is in the box. He can even be pressured to change the way he walks, talks, or dresses to be more "manly."

If a young woman is strong, athletic, smart, not interested in boys, good at mechanics or math, or won't put up with male abuse, she can be pressured by being called a dyke or lesbian.

Discuss with the class that, in fact, our sexual orientation is not something we choose but something we discover as we grow older. Some of us know that we are lesbian, gay, bisexual, or heterosexual at an early age. Some of us don't develop a sexual orientation until later in our lives. Many of us are questioning our sexuality even now.

Wherever we are in the process—regardless of our sexual orientation—every single one of us has the right to lead lives free of harassment, intimidation, pressure, and abuse. Homophobia contributes directly to keeping us all in our boxes and to enforcing gender roles. Any campaign to make the peace—regardless of our personal feelings about people with sexual orientations different from ours—must include the safety to be ourselves, publicly, without having to hide who we are to avoid abuse.

The "One Thing" Exercise

Explain that in the following exercise you would like the young women to participate and the men to just listen, without comments, laughter, or other response. Tell the young men that if this gets hard for them, they can just notice what feelings they have about listening to young women talk. Then, say to the young women in the class:

What is one thing that men or boys say to you—something that hurts you or that you don't like—that you never want to hear again?

Write their comments on the board.

> One Thing
>
> trust me
> if you loved me you would
> I'll call you
> you'll do what I tell you
> you're my woman
> no fat chicks allowed

What is this list of things that men or boys say to you telling you about how you are supposed to act as a woman? What in your upbringing have you learned about how you are supposed to act if you are a "good girl"? What does society tell you to do to "act like a lady"?

Act-Like-a-Lady Box

List the students' responses on the board about "how women are supposed to act." Draw a box around this list.

Act Like a Lady

> sweet
> sexy, but not too sexy
> passive
> listener
> smart, but not too smart
> caretaker

Making the Peace

We call this the Act-Like-a-Lady Box. Just like in the Act-Like-a-Man Box, girls and women get called names to make them stay in this box, to make them act the way society says "nice girls" and "nice women" should act. What names do girls or women get called if they try to step out of the box?

Explain that women get called different names for being out of the box in different ways. Maybe if, according to the box, a woman is "too smart," she will be called a bitch. If a woman is "overly provocative" according to society, she might be called one of the "whore" words. If a woman is "too athletic" for the box, she might be called a dyke. Write the words that students suggest along the right side of the box. Draw a fist around the list, and label it "verbal abuse."

You may have noticed that a lot of the names guys get called have to do with being tough, about what guys do. What do you notice about a lot of the names that women get called? (Most of them are about women being—or not being—sexual. Women are typically identified with sexual behavior and how they look.)

How about these names? (Point out dyke, les, and other terms referring to lesbians.) What happens to girls or women who want close relationships of any kind with other women? What message do you get about lesbians from these names? Why are these names used?

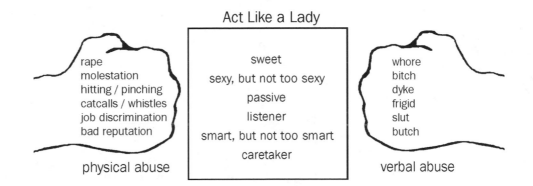

Act Like a Lady

physical abuse		verbal abuse
rape	sweet	whore
molestation	sexy, but not too sexy	bitch
hitting / pinching	passive	dyke
catcalls / whistles	listener	frigid
job discrimination	smart, but not too smart	slut
bad reputation	caretaker	butch

Next, ask the group to tell you some of the things that get done to women because of their gender. Write this list along the left side of the box. Draw a fist around the list, and label it "physical abuse."

Explain that women are often led to believe that they will be safe if they stay in the box because men will protect them. This is a lie: girls and women can be raped or beaten regardless of whether they are in the box or not, just by virtue of being female. The statistic is that one out of three or four girls is sexually abused by the time she is 18— usually by an adult male. And one out of three teenage women in a dating relationship in high school gets physically or sexually abused.

Training boys and girls to behave like the Act-Like-a-Man and Act-Like-a-Lady boxes tell them to is a primary way that sexism—male power over women—is maintained. Like other forms of violence, sexism is eventually internalized. Many women come to believe the messages that they hear again and again—that they are not real women unless they are wild about and submissive to men, or unless they are pretty, thin, blond, blue-eyed, and dependent, and love taking care of other people. To cope with the pressures of having to live in the box—and the physical and sexual violence and harassment that many young women face—some turn to self-destructive actions such as drugs, suicide, running away from home, eating disorders, or high-risk sexual activity.

Distribute Handouts 15 and 16. Ask students to fill in the Act-Like-a-Lady Box, adding their own words. Ask them to notice in the next few days the messages that women are given and to add other words to the handout. Give them a few more minutes to review the handout on sexism.

As a class, discuss this question: How have any women you know challenged sexism?

Closure

To close this session, explain that if we are going to make the peace, we must make the peace between men and women. This means challenging the violence that men do to women in our own lives and in the community around us. The media often focus on the violence that men do to other men, and on the danger to women from strangers. However, the greatest danger to women of any age is physical and sexual abuse from men they know—fathers, stepfathers, boyfriends, coworkers.

Women need to know that if they are abused, they are not to blame, and that there are many places they can go to get help. Men need to know that they have no right to control, harass, or abuse women. Abusive men need to see other men challenging the abuse, and they need to know that they too can get help. We will continue analyzing this topic in the next session.

Distribute On Your Own sheet 7 (for the young men only), sheet 8 (for the young women only), and sheet 9.

Tonight's homework is in two parts. First, you will each get a list of categories—one list if you are a woman, the other if you are a man—about how young women and men get raised. Read through the list and answer the questions at the bottom of the page. We will talk about the lists in the next session. Second, observe male and female relationships around you. Notice when people are in the boxes and when they are stepping out. Bring in examples from the media and interactions you observe, and describe how each situation fits in the boxes or challenges the boxes. Look carefully for examples of people stepping out of the boxes, because those are more difficult to find.

What if . . .

Some students challenge the acceptance of lesbians, gays, or bisexuals as worthy of respect and safety? The students may raise questions based on religious, family, or community values, or based on misinformation they have received through the media about homosexuality, AIDS, or other issues. Without getting into a more extended discussion of their concerns, the two most important points to emphasize are that (1) lesbian, gay, and bisexual people are a part of our community and deserve the same respect and safety that everyone has a right to, and (2) homophobia keeps us all—regardless of our sexual orientation—locked into the rigid boxes of behavior and encourages men to be violent to prove they are tough. We can't make the peace if some of us are the targets of violence.

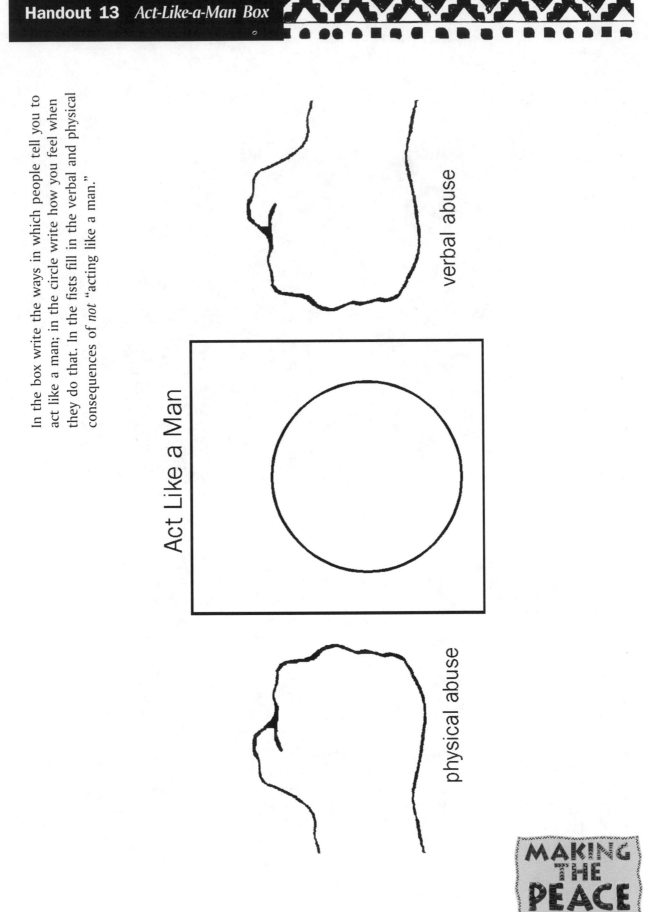

In the box write the ways in which people tell you to act like a man; in the circle write how you feel when they do that. In the fists fill in the verbal and physical consequences of *not* "acting like a man."

verbal abuse

Act Like a Man

physical abuse

MAKING THE PEACE

What it is

Heterosexism is the exploitation, mistreatment, and abuse of lesbian, gay, and bisexual people. *Homophobia* is the fear of homosexuals and the fear of being gay or of being thought to be gay.

Who it affects

Everyone, particularly people who are lesbian, gay, or bisexual.

How it is enforced

School, housing, and job discrimination; physical and sexual assault; police brutality; inadequate health care; criminalization of nonheterosexual activity; stereotypes and misinformation on TV, in the movies, and in popular culture; expulsion from families when individuals come out as homosexual; the expectation that everyone is naturally and normally heterosexual; forcing people to keep their sexual orientation a secret.

How it might look at school

Gay-bashing; use of gay-baiting (calling people *fag* or *wimp* to get them to fight); pressure for every-one to be in straight couples and sexually involved; lack of visibility of lesbian, gay, and bisexual leadership and role models at the administrative, teacher, and student levels; lack of information about sexuality and sexual orientation for young people; lack of recreational facilities or safe places for lesbian, gay, and bisexual youth to congregate.

How it is internalized

Violence against peers: Isolation and separation from others who are lesbian, gay, and bisexual; gossip and rumors; competition.

Self-destructive violence: Self-blame; apathy; despair; suicide; drug use; high-risk sexual activity; eating disorders.

Who can be allies

Every heterosexual person can be an ally to lesbians, gays, and bisexuals. Lesbians, gays, and bisexu-als can be allies to each other.

How it has been resisted

Lesbians, gays, and bisexuals have provided leadership for most struggles for social change without being visible for who they are. They have been leaders in women's, disabled rights, students', labor, civil rights, and other movements. They have created a culture of resistance including music, art, literature, and popular culture.

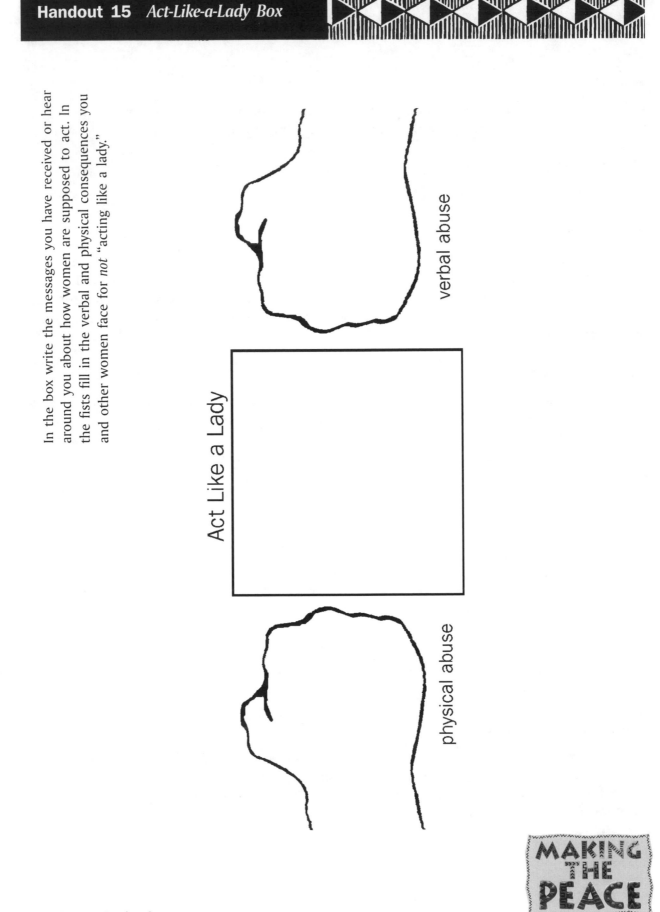

In the box write the messages you have received or hear around you about how women are supposed to act. In the fists fill in the verbal and physical consequences you and other women face for *not* "acting like a lady."

verbal abuse

Act Like a Lady

physical abuse

MAKING THE PEACE

What it is

Sexism is systematic exploitation, mistreatment, and abuse of women by men.

Who it affects

Everyone, particularly women and girls.

How it is enforced

Dating and family physical violence; date rape and incest; sexual harassment on the job and in the streets; teasing, put-downs, and stereotypes; lack of visibility of women in leadership, women role models, and women's concerns in television and film; less pay than men for equal work; unequal health care; lack of representation in social, political, economic, and legal institutions.

How it might look at school

Predominantly male leadership at administrative, teacher, or student levels; lack of safety for women on campus; unequal funding for women's activities (such as sports); sexual harassment in the classroom; tracking of young women into traditional jobs, careers, or activities; invisibility of women in history, math, science, and literature; sexual assault on and off campus; physical violence in dating relationships.

How it is internalized

Violence against peers: Fights between young women; competition, gossip, and rumors about other young women; put-downs of women's achievements; supporting men's abusive behavior; separation from other women.

Self-destructive violence: Self-blame; apathy; hopelessness; drug use; suicide; eating disorders; high-risk physical and sexual activity; prostitution; gangs; obsessive attention to appearance.

Who can be allies

Every man can be an ally to women. Women can be allies to each other.

How it has been resisted

Women have been leaders in every struggle for human freedom, justice, and equality, including women's, civil rights, disability, lesbian and gay, and labor movements. Women have organized rape centers and battered women's shelters and fought for homeless aid, child care, and better social services for all people. They have created women's literature, music, organizations, and political campaigns to challenge the status quo.

Read each category below, and ask yourself if this has happened to you—or to a man your age you know.

1. Have you ever worried that you weren't tough enough?

2. Have you ever exercised to make yourself tougher?

3. Were you ever told not to cry?

4. Were you ever hit to make you stop crying?

5. Have you ever been called a wimp, a queer, or a fag?

6. Have you ever been told to act like a man?

7. Have you ever been hit by an older man?

8. Have you ever been forced to fight, or been in a fight because you felt you had to prove you were a man?

9. Did you ever see an adult man you looked up to or respected hit or emotionally abuse a woman?

10. Have you ever been physically injured by another person?

11. Have you ever been physically injured and hid the pain or kept it to yourself?

12. Have you stopped yourself from showing affection to, hugging, or touching another man because of how it might look?

13. Have you ever been touched in a way you didn't like by an older person?

14. Have you ever been arrested or done time in jail or prison or the juvenile justice system?

15. Did you ever drink or take drugs to cover your feelings or hide your pain?

16. Have you ever felt like killing yourself?

17. Do you have any scars on your body from knife or bullet wounds?

18. Have you ever had your life threatened by another man?

19. Do you know, or are you a friend of someone who knows, a man who was killed by another man?

20. Have you ever engaged in sexual activity with a girl or woman when she didn't want to?

21. Have you ever been sexually molested?

How does it feel to read these categories? What do they tell us about how boys are taught to be men?

Read each category below, and ask yourself if this has happened to you—or to a woman your age you know.

1. Have you ever worn makeup, shaved your legs or underarms, or worn nylons?

2. Have you ever worn uncomfortable, restrictive clothing—heels, a girdle, clothes that felt too tight or too revealing?

3. Have you ever worried that you were not pretty enough?

4. Have you ever felt you were not feminine enough?

5. Have you ever changed your diet or exercised to change your body size, shape, or weight?

6. Have you ever felt less important than a man?

7. Have you ever pretended to be less intelligent than you are to protect a boy's or man's ego?

8. Did you ever remain silent, or were you ever ignored, because boys or men were doing all the talking?

9. Have you ever felt limited in what careers are open to you?

10. Have you ever been sexually pressured by a boy or man in your school, church, workplace, or other public place?

11. Were you were ever yelled at, commented on, whistled at, touched, or harassed by a boy or man in a public place?

12. Have you have ever been called a bitch, a slut, a whore, or a similar name?

13. Have you ever limited your activity, or changed your plans to go somewhere, out of fear for your physical safety from men?

14. Do you routinely alter your plans or limit your activity because of fear for your physical safety from boys or men?

15. Have you ever stopped yourself from showing affection to, hugging, or touching another woman because of how it might look?

16. Have you ever been afraid of a man's anger?

17. Have you ever said yes to a man because you were afraid to say no?

18. Have you ever been pressured to engage in sexual activity with a boy or man when you didn't want to?

19. Have you ever been hit by a man?

20. Have you ever been sexually molested?

How does it feel to read these categories? What do they tell us about how girls are trained to be women?

Between now and the next session, describe one song, one TV program, one advertisement, and one interaction between people and state how it either reinforces the boxes or is a challenge to them.

Song description:

Analysis:

TV program description:

Analysis:

Advertisement description:

Analysis:

Interaction between people description:

Analysis:

Women and Men Together (continued)

Preparation

■ Review the step-out exercises on pages 122–124. Decide which categories are appropriate to use, keeping them arranged in order from the least to the most severe form of violence.

■ You will need copies of Handout 17 and On Your Own sheet 10. Have the "boxes" you drew in Session 9 available for reference.

To Begin: Review of Gender Training and Sexism

In your own words, briefly review what the group has already explored about the issues of gender training and sexism in our society.

In the last session, we looked at how boys and girls are trained to be men and women. We saw that male and female roles are taught to us as children and enforced by teasing, harassment, threats, and abuse. We also saw that part of that training is about sexism—the mistreatment of people because of their gender, especially women by men. And part of it is about homophobia and heterosexism—if any of us are the least bit uncomfortable in those boxes, or show the slightest inclination to step out, we will be challenged and pressured to prove we are heterosexual. That puts everyone who is lesbian, gay, or bisexual in danger of being the target of harassment, put-downs, and abuse. It also makes it more dangerous for everyone—gay or straight—who challenges the roles or takes leadership in any action for change.

Today we will explore how men and women can work together to prevent violence against women. First, we want to examine a little more deeply the costs of these gender roles on our lives. Part of the last homework was for you to look over the lists of ways men and women sometimes get treated.

Allow students a few minutes to share what the lists made them think about, and also what they noticed from doing the exercise on observing sexism in their immediate surroundings.

Step-Out Exercises

Explain that the group will now do an exercise that involves some of the first few categories from the lists. Have the young men and women line up on opposite sides of the room, facing each other. Explain that the following exercise will be done in two parts, first for the young men and then for the young women. The exercise should be done silently. If students feel the need to talk, laugh, or make noise, ask them to notice the uncomfortable feelings they are experiencing rather than to express them and distract others. The gender group that is watching at the time should be particularly respectful, because this is not an easy exercise. Remind students of the Agreements on respect, listening, and confidentiality. Also explain that although everyone must participate in the exercise, individuals may choose to pass for any particular question.

Men's Step-Out

Read each statement you have selected, and ask all the male students to whom it applies to take two steps forward, notice who else has stepped forward, and notice their feelings. Then ask them to step back into line, and then read the next statement. Ask the young women to remain silent and to respect the men's space. Remind the men that they have the right to pass on a particular category if they feel they need to.

Please step forward silently if

1. You have ever worried that you were not tough enough.

2. You have ever exercised to make yourself tougher.

3. You were ever told not to cry.

4. You were ever hit to make you stop crying.

5. You have ever been called a wimp, a queer, or a fag.

6. You have ever been told to act like a man.

7. You have ever been hit by an older man.

8. You have ever been forced to fight, or been in a fight because you felt you had to prove you were a man.

9. You ever saw an adult man you looked up to or respected hit or emotionally abuse a woman.

10. You have ever been physically injured by another person.

11. You have ever been physically injured and hid the pain or kept it to yourself.

12. You ever stopped yourself from showing affection, hugging, or touching another man because of how it might look.

Women's Step-Out

After the last men's category has been called, turn to the women's line. Ask the women to follow the same procedure, and ask the men to remain silent and respect the women's space. Remind the women that they have the right to pass on a particular question if they feel they need to.

Please step forward silently if

1. You have ever worried that you were not pretty or feminine enough.

2. You have ever worn uncomfortable, restrictive clothing—heels, a girdle, clothes that felt too tight or too revealing.

3. You have ever worn makeup, shaved your legs or underarms, or worn nylons.

4. You ever changed your diet or exercised to change your body size, shape, or weight.

5. You have ever felt less important than a man.

6. You have ever pretended to be less intelligent than you are to protect a boy's or a man's ego.

7. You have ever remained silent, or were ever ignored, because boys or men were doing all the talking.

8. You have ever felt limited in what careers are open to you.

9. You were ever sexually pressured by a boy or a man in your school, church, workplace, or other public place.

10. You were ever yelled at, commented on, whistled at, touched, or harassed by a boy or man in a public place.

11. You have ever been called a bitch, a slut, a whore, or a similar name.

12. You have ever limited your activity, or changed your plans to go somewhere, out of fear for your physical safety from men.

13. You routinely alter your plans or limit your activity because of fear for your physical safety from boys or men.

14. You have ever said yes to a man because you were afraid to say no.

Have the group break into same-gender pairs to discuss the feelings that arose during the step-out exercise.

Violence Against Women

Reassemble the group, and distribute Handout 17.

Everyone is hurt by sexism and rigid gender roles. However, women are almost 20 times more likely to be victims of male violence than men are to be victims of violence from women. When men get hurt, it is usually by other men. To make the peace, we must stop male violence—in particular, violence against women.

On the handout, take a few minutes to describe a time when you witnessed violence against a woman. If you are a woman, you may instead describe a time when you experienced it directly.

If time allows, ask for a few volunteers to recount their experiences.

Sexual Harassment

When we see a woman being abused by a man, we can certainly intervene directly. We will talk more about such intervention in later sessions.

One way to make it safer for women in our society is to create a climate in which women are respected. To do that, we must stop sexual harassment. What is sexual harassment?

Take several answers, then offer the following definition and write it on the board: Sexual harassment is any type of unwelcome, threatening, or intimidating conduct directed toward a student or employee because of his or her gender.

Explain that, under this definition, sexual harassment has been experienced by between 85 and 89 percent of high-school-age women, according to four national surveys conducted in the last few years. Then, introduce the next activity.

We are going to consider two scenarios and brainstorm how we might make the peace when sexual harassment is occurring—first when an individual is involved, and then when a group is doing the harassing.

Read aloud each of the scenarios below. After each scenario ask the group the discussion questions that follow.

Scenario A   John often makes comments about the girls in the class—how they are dressed, and what he thinks of their bodies. He also makes comments about some of the guys, calling them geeks, wimps, and fags, and making jokes about their sexual experience and ability.

Scenario B   A group of young men hangs out by some lockers in the hall and makes comments about all the girls who walk past, rating their bodies on a scale of 1 to 10.

Discussion questions

- Is this sexual harassment?

- What can students, individually or as a group, do about it?

If time allows, break students into two groups, one for each scenario. Ask the groups to brainstorm how they could, as a group, successfully intervene to stop the harassment. Have them role-play intervention strategies to practice them and to gauge their effectiveness.

If you do not have enough time for the groupwork, move directly to these closing questions for the entire class:

■ Where does sexual harassment happen, in any form, in this school?

■ How can young men be allies of young women in dealing with sexual harassment in this school?

Encourage the young women to describe what kind of support they need from young men. Ask the young men to describe, concretely, what they could do to be better allies to young women.

Closure

To close the session, emphasize once more the necessity of men and women making the peace.

To make an effective peace, men and women must be able to work together. And we can only do that if we acknowledge how much sexism costs all of us, and how sexual violence makes each of us vulnerable.

It is not easy to look at or talk about these issues, and I appreciate your attention, energy, and honesty. If issues came up for you today that feel unresolved, please find someone you trust to talk with about them. Take care of yourselves. Bring any other feelings, questions, or thoughts you have about these issues to the next session, when we can continue our discussion.

Distribute On Your Own sheet 10, and respond to any questions about it.

What if . . .

Some male students (and some young women) blame women for male violence? Students may make such comments as, "Some girls ask for it," or "Why don't women leave if they don't like it?" It is important to emphasize that no one wants or asks to be hurt. No one invites pain and abuse. The questions we should be asking instead are, "Why does he hit her?" or "Why does he assume that because she dresses a certain way, he can force her to have sex with him?" Sexism, like all oppression, works by blaming the victims for causing the violence that happens to them—thus conveniently shifting attention away from the perpetrators of the violence; in this case, men. You can also draw parallels to other categories on the Power Chart and the ways in which young people, workers, and people of color are blamed for the violence they receive from adults, bosses, and white people, respectively.

Describe an incident when you saw a man being violent to a woman. If you are a woman, you may describe a time you experienced violence from a man. Briefly describe what happened, what you felt at the time, and how it has affected you.

MAKING
THE
PEACE

If you are a female, name and describe one woman in your life—or one woman historically—who has been a role model for you of a strong, powerful, caring woman who stepped out of the box.

If you are male, name and describe one man in your life—or one man historically—who has been a role model for you of a strong, powerful, caring man who stepped out of the box and was an ally to women.

Making the Peace Now

Sessions 11, 12, and 13 deal with the immediate violence that students might be facing. Each session is designed to help students identify and assess situations of danger, develop safety plans and strategies for changing those situations, and learn how to support each other in stopping violence. These sessions will begin to give students a practical sense of how they can come together to make the peace, and how significant a difference it can make in their lives and their school when they do.

Session 14 revisits the concept of being allies to solidify students' commitment to becoming involved in making the peace. Realistic strategies for dealing with violent situations are also explored. Session 15 looks at how students can continue the work and organizing they have begun in these sessions.

Guns and Violence

Aims

- To assess the current incidence of violence in and effects of guns and other weapons on school and family life

- To identify strategies for getting help to address weapon use on campus, at home, and in the community

- To identify patterns and behaviors that make it difficult to get help

- To plan ahead for dealing with potential violence involving weapons

Skills

Students will

- Identify actual and potential violence they experience related to guns and other weapons such as knives

- Identify help and resources for dealing with guns and other weapons

- Identify personal and social barriers to getting help and finding resources

- Make a safety plan to cope immediately with the presence of weapons in the community

Preparation

- Review the section on guns in the Introduction (see page 25). Select two student facilitators, a young woman and a young man, to facilitate the gun agreement discussion. Have the Agreements posted in preparation for the addition of the gun agreement. You will need copies of On Your Own sheet 11.

To Begin: Overview on Guns

Introduce the topic of this session: guns and violence. Tell students that the purpose of this session is not to lecture them about guns, but to help them think about how they are affected by guns and what they can do to keep themselves safe.

Note: **If you suspect that guns are present in your classroom, do not conduct this session, as discussions about guns could be extremely unsafe in this environment. Instead, pursue the procedures your school has in place to remove suspected weapons. You may want to discuss what happened as a group later in the program.**

Ask students what they know or have heard about gun use and violence among young people in the United States, both other-directed and self-directed. Write their responses on the board. Make sure these general questions are addressed:

- Who is hurt by guns?

- Who uses guns?

- How much gun violence—injury, homicide, and suicide—is there?

- What kinds of guns are used most often?

- Where do people get guns?

- Who makes money from guns?

Take a few minutes to pull together the various responses. If needed, add the following facts to the discussion:

- Guns are one of the primary causes of death of young people your age in the United States; 20 times as many young people die from gunshots in the U.S. as in the next eight countries combined.

- Over twice as many teenagers ages 15 to 19 are being killed by guns as were ten years ago.

- Guns are used in three out of five youth suicides and in four out of five youth homicides.

- A gun in the home is 43 times more likely to kill a family member or friend than anyone else (for example, someone a family member shoots in self-defense).

- The sale of guns for domestic use is a large, profitable industry in the United States. In 1990, gun manufacturers produced 12,000 guns per day. The U.S. is also the largest supplier of guns to developing countries.

- In California, where there is one McDonald's for every 3,500 people, there is one gun dealer for every 1,000 people.

Continue the discussion by asking students these general questions:

■ Where do you see guns? (Encourage students to think not only of real guns, but of play guns and guns in film, video, and television, video and computer games, and cartoons and comic books.)

■ When was last time you held a toy gun or a real gun of any kind in your hand, or had your finger on a trigger, like in a video game? Briefly describe the experience, and how you felt doing it.

■ What is it about guns that attracts people or makes them feel powerful?

■ What is it about guns that frightens people?

■ What might make it hard to talk about guns in this group?

At the end of this discussion, break the class into groups of three or four for small-group discussions.

Small-Group Discussions

Choose one of the two formats below for conducting the small-group discussions. If the last question in the class discussion seemed to bring up feelings of fear or hesitation, have groups do the "Best Thinking" Exercise; otherwise, choose the Personal Stories option. Whichever you choose, emphasize that each member of the group will get equal time to talk (between 3 and 5 minutes, to be timed by you).

Introduce the exercise, and give students a few minutes to think about their response before starting to time the response segments.

Personal Stories

This exercise is intended to give students time to reflect on the role that guns play in their lives. Write the categories on the board for students to refer to.

When it is your turn to speak, please tell the group about an experience, positive or negative, that you have had with guns at home, in your neighborhood, or at school. I would like you to relate:

■ what happened

■ what you did about it

■ how you felt about what happened

■ what you would do differently now, if anything.

"Best Thinking" Exercise

This exercise is a group process that encourages critical thinking and problem solving. It allows each person an opportunity to think about and analyze a volatile issue, while everyone else in the group listens attentively. Write the three questions below on the board for students to refer to.

When it is your turn to speak, please tell the group your thoughts on this issue:

- What are the costs and benefits to an individual person of that person having a gun?
- What are the costs and benefits to the surrounding community?
- Given the presence of guns in our community, what next steps can be taken to make the peace?

If there is time, have each group briefly share what was covered in that group.

Problem-Solving Role Plays

Pair up the small groups to form larger groups of six to eight members. Explain that each group is to create a role play of a situation involving gun use at home, in the neighborhood, or at school in which someone is using or threatening to use a gun, or someone is frightened by the potential for gun use by someone else. You might specify which group will address guns in the home, which one guns in the neighborhood, and which one guns at school. Give the students these guidelines:

1. Each role play is to have two different endings. The first ending is what, in the group's experience, usually happens when this scenario with guns occurs. The second ending is their "best thinking," as a group, about how to end the scenario safely and practically so as to remove or neutralize the threat of guns.

2. The role play must be something that could really happen.

3. The role play must have a role for each group member.

4. If the role play involves any physical contact between students, the students must agree to and practice the contact to ensure physical safety.

5. "Safely and practically" ending the role play means just that: the successful ending must ultimately be nonviolent (that is, it must not "deny human integrity"), it must not be superhuman, and it must create or preserve safety.

Role Play Presentation

Depending on the time available, have one or two groups present their role plays. Have groups follow these steps:

1. Describe what the role play is about.

2. Present the first version of the role play.

3. Allow members of the audience to respond to the role play by describing what they saw and what they think would help to end the role play safely.

4. Present the second version.

Lead the audience in applause for the performers.

The Gun Agreement

Display the original Agreements. As a group, talk about adding a new agreement to the list. This "Gun Agreement" would be a safety agreement that students are willing to make with each other to promote comfort and eliminate gun use in the group. Add the new agreement to the posted Agreement list.

If there is time, have student facilitators conduct the class through a brainstorming exercise in which the class answers the following questions in the areas of "home," "neighborhood," and "school."

- How are our homes, neighborhoods, and school affected negatively by the presence of guns?

- What should we do in the next 30 days to deal with the presence of guns in each of these areas?

- What should we do to decrease gun violence in each of these areas in the coming year?

Closure

Pass out On Your Own sheet 11, and answer any questions about it.

Making the Peace

What if . . .

Some students contend that guns are necessary for self-defense or self-protection? Invite them to talk about safety itself: How safe do they feel in the presence of guns? How unsafe do they feel in the presence of guns? Fully acknowledge the importance of and right to self-protection, but open the discussion up for less dangerous ways to secure safety.

Students report or have stories about guns in their homes? It may be important to distinguish between guns for "recreational use," such as hunting or target shooting, and guns kept for offensive purposes, self-defense, or safety. Note the danger firearms pose in all households regardless of their intended purpose. You may want to ask discussion questions, such as: How do you feel about guns in your homes? What steps might help secure these guns against misuse?

You suspect there are guns in your classroom? It is very likely your students also suspect—or know—that guns are present. **This will make any discussion extremely unsafe—omit this session entirely.** Pursue the procedures your school has in place to remove suspected weapons. If you go through such a process, it may be appropriate to make time later in the series to discuss what happened.

Make a list of every place you have seen an image of a gun, seen a gun used, or heard someone refer to guns—outside of today's class—in the last 24 hours. This includes references to guns on television, videos, radio, and the news, and in comics, newspapers, and magazines.

Look over your list. What does it tell you about guns? What messages does it give you? How does it make you feel?

Think of an incident involving someone you know being threatened or injured with a gun. What happened? What kind of gun was it, and where do you think it came from? What happened as a result of the incident? What might have prevented it?

Picture your neighborhood, your school, and the surrounding region. Draw a rough outline of the area on the back of this sheet. If someone wanted a gun, where would he or she go? If you can, mark on your outline where—inside and outside your region—someone could obtain a gun. Include friends, family members, gun stores, mail-order catalogues, and illegal sources.

   Next, mark any areas in your region where you know or have heard that guns are used and that people are hurt by guns.

Self-Directed Violence

Aims

- To help students heal from self-directed abuse

- To give students an understanding of self-destructive violence and its effects on school and family life

- To encourage students to get help for self-destructive behavior

- To support students reaching out to one another

Skills

Students will

- Identify actual and potential self-directed violence they participate in or see around them

- Identify realistic help and useable resources for dealing with self-directed violence

- Reach out to and support each other

- Learn and practice intervention skills

Preparation

- You will need copies of Handout 18. You will also need the heart diagram and the Power Chart from Session 2.

To Begin: Overview on Self-Directed Violence

Briefly review the conclusions the group came to after doing the Heart Exercise in Session 2.

All human beings are born intelligent, eager, loving, and good. And, all human beings bruise and scar very easily.

Make the connection from the scarred heart to the possibility of self-directed violence.

In a society in which there is so much violence, and in which our own hearts have been hurt, it is easy to become discouraged and depressed and to blame ourselves for what happens to us. If we someday reach a point when we no longer believe there is anything to live for, we may become self-destructive—in other words, we may become violent toward ourselves. Many people who would never think of hurting someone else are very skilled at hurting themselves.

It is not unusual to feel sad or depressed occasionally. However, being seriously depressed or dwelling on thoughts of hurting yourself, making plans to hurt yourself, or doing self-destructive things is definitely cause for concern. If you find yourself doing any of these things, you need support from those you can trust to pull through the difficult times . . . to help you heal your heart.

Analysis of Self-Destructive Behavior

As a group, brainstorm a list of the many ways that people can be self-destructive.

In what ways can people hurt themselves, or be destructive toward their bodies, or risk their future?

As students offer suggestions, make a list on the board. Make sure that eating disorders, high-speed driving, dangerous sports, drugs, abusive relationships, and suicide are among the items on the list.

Display the Power Chart. Then, referring to lines on the Power Chart, ask questions to get students thinking about the sources of these self-destructive behaviors.

How can racism lead a person to give up hope and become self-destructive? How can lack of economic opportunity lead to destructive behavior? How about gender-role pressure and sexism? How about homophobia?

Ask for specific responses for each question, and then turn the conversation toward young people.

Specifically, how can adultism cause young people to internalize the hurt, discrimination, and blame from adults and begin to hurt themselves?

Once students have discussed this question, explain that when people want to hurt themselves it is often because the past has been so painful that they forget that the future can be better. They lose touch with other people, with the simple pleasures of life, with the possibility of a better tomorrow. They begin to believe that nobody cares about them and that, therefore, it is OK not to care about themselves.

Sharing of Personal Experiences

Distribute Handout 18 and explain that it is about self-destructive violence in our own lives.

Think about times in your life when you were discouraged and perhaps thought about doing, or did, something self-destructive. What did you really need at that time in your life? Please take several minutes to answer the questions on this handout.

Give students six to eight minutes to answer the questions. Then, organize the students into groups of three.

In your groups, I want you to talk about (1) what you needed in the situation you wrote about, and (2) someone who was really able to reach you when you needed help. Please describe who that person was and what they did to help you. Each of you will have two minutes to talk.

When students have finished sharing their experiences, convey the following in your own words:

When people hurt themselves intentionally, it is usually because they are experiencing such strong feelings of grief, sadness, anger, or pain that they feel overwhelmed. It seems easier to them to try to hide the pain and other feelings than to experience them. They may turn to alcohol or other drugs, abuse their bodies, live dangerously, or try to end their lives in an attempt to deny or escape the painful reality that caused them their feelings.

We don't need to face these situations alone. But it sometimes takes a lot of courage to admit that we are vulnerable, that we need help to get through the hard times. When someone is being self-destructive they are hurting inside, regardless of how tough, carefree, uncaring, or invulnerable they try to appear. Knowing this, we can sometimes tell when people are being self-destructive, and we can reach out to them.

Guidelines for Intervention

As a class, list on the board what methods or actions might work to reach people who are being self-destructive. Then, organize the list into the following five guidelines:

1. Listen and confirm.

Help them talk about what they are feeling. Acknowledge the pain, isolation, or depression they are experiencing. Don't try to convince them that everything is really all right.

2. Show them you care.

Show them you care, and assure them that you will help them get through this tough time. Let them know you would be sad if they weren't around.

3. Remind them of the heart.

Help remind them of things they enjoy in their lives and things they have to look forward to.

4. Provide perspective.

Remind them that things *always* change and that they can get better.

5. Help them locate support systems.

Find or help them find hotline numbers, a counselor, books, or other sources of support.

"Lean on Me" Role Plays

Divide the class into groups of five or six and have each group do a role play, using one of the three scenarios below.

In each of the three scenarios, one student plays a person who is self-destructive, and another plays his or her friend. The object of the role play is for the friend to help the self-destructive person stop hurting herself or himself. Several people could play the friend in turn for each scene to give several students a chance to try out intervention strategies. Students might try serious talking, humor, distractions, just listening, or sharing their own experiences of sadness or hurt.

Scenario A

A person is using alcohol or other drugs a lot.

Scenario B

A person is anorexic or bulimic and visibly unhealthy.

Scenario C

A person is talking as though they have no reason to keep on living.

After groups have practiced their role plays, reconvene the class and have groups volunteer to present their role plays. After each scenario is played out, ask the person who is self-destructive to talk about what he or she needed. Have the group identify what the friend did that was helpful. Then ask the group to think about what else might have worked. Don't let the group focus on what didn't work in the intervention. Convey that it is always important to take chances and to reach out, even if we make mistakes.

Closure

Take a few moments for any personal reflections from students or appreciation they have for other students for something they did or said during the session. Then, summarize what the group has explored.

Self-destructive violence is part of the cycle of violence that we are trying to eliminate. We can only do that when each person has support, friends to talk with, respect, a safe environment, and a clear sense of their own future. We must learn how to care for each other, because the loss of any one of us is a loss to all of us. Reaching out is the opposite of violence. To make the peace we must replace isolation, separation, and lack of concern for each other with caring and active support.

What if...

A student tells you she is engaged in some form of self-abuse or is thinking about suicide? What is to be done immediately, in the short term? When a student imparts such information to you, she or he is clearly asking for some kind of help. Even a joking reference to self-abuse or suicide signals some unease on the student's part and a need for adult witness.

If the student indicates this in the presence of other students, she may be asking you and them both for some attention; if she tells you in private, she may want to talk with you alone. In either case, it is very important to set a time relatively promptly to talk to her about what she has said. After the class, or after school that day, you can talk with her or set a time then to talk. Decide whether it is appropriate to involve friends of hers. You might encourage her to bring a best friend her age whom she trusts to keep confidentiality. Make sure to acknowledge what she says—to let her know that you have heard her, and to clarify in detail, by asking her direct questions, what she is thinking about. Every reference is to be taken seriously; at the same time, it is not to be taken heavy-handedly; you want to convey the sense that plenty of time can be made to talk these things through.

Professional counselors who talk with adolescents about suicide put a high value on the practical—asking the student exactly what actions he is contemplating ("Are you thinking of killing yourself?"), whether he has a weapon, whether he has picked a time when he is planning to hurt or kill himself. The more detail a student provides in answer to these questions, the higher the likelihood that abuse or suicide will happen.

In the longer term, of course, you and the student will need other resources. You can't rescue another person from hurting themselves; the attempt to do so isolates you and leaves the student without skills to build his own support network. And it leaves you unavailable for other students who may be asking for your help less directly.

Build *your* support network ahead of time, just as you are training students in this session to do. Consult with school counselors and your best teacher friend before the class to think about what might come up. Bring the list of counselors, local hotlines, and support groups to pass on to any student who is asking for help. Always take what is said to you seriously and concretely, and as soon as you can, bring other adults and the student's best friends into the process.

Write about a time you did something self-destructive or thought about doing something self-destructive. What was it that you really needed at that time? What got you through that period?

Is there anything you are doing now that is self-destructive? Why do you think you are putting your health or life at risk? Who gains from this? Who loses? Name one person you could talk with about this.

What things in your life now are worth living for?

What's Going On Now?

Aims

- To assess the current incidence of violence and effects of gender issues, race, drugs, weapons, and gangs on school and family life

- To identify strategies for getting help to stop current violence

- To identify patterns and behaviors that make it difficult to get help

- To plan ahead for dealing with immediate violence

Skills

Students will

- Identify current actual and potential violence they experience

- Identify realistic help and resources for dealing with violence

- Identify personal and social barriers to getting help and finding resources

- Make a safety plan to cope with immediate violence

Preparation

- You will need copies of Handout 19 and On Your Own sheet 12.

To Begin: Overview on Immediate Violence

Take a few moments to review the Agreements on page 49. Ask for any thoughts or feelings students want to share about the previous session's topic.

During the last few sessions, we have been looking very closely at our personal experiences of violence. Some of you may have identified a relationship you have right now in which you could be or are being hurt or put down; in which you could be or are hurting someone else; in which you could hurt or are hurting yourself. Now it's time for us to help each other find ways to be safer.

Part of making the peace is taking care of ourselves: getting the help we need from friends, family, and allies to be safe and free of fear. You deserve to be completely safe. You deserve total respect from those around you. You have the right to get help whenever you need it.

Ask students to think about an experience of violence in their lives right now—something being done to them or something they are doing to someone else or to themselves. The experience might involve someone being threatened or put down, yelled at, pushed, hit, beaten, abused, discriminated against, ignored, or made to feel afraid—whether it seems serious or not. Assure students that they will not have to say what they are thinking of out loud.

When you think of an experience, raise your hand.

Let a few moments of silence pass. When most or all hands are raised, say:

That's what we will be thinking about today.

Identifying Violence Role Plays

Distribute Handout 19, and allow students several minutes to complete it.

Then break students into groups of three or four. In their groups, students will identify violent, or potentially violent, situations that typically involve students, and they will talk about strategies for getting help to stop the violence.

Referring to the handout, choose one type of violence to focus on. With your group, script out a role play of a typical situation involving that type of violence. Talk about possible ways for the person being abused to respond. Practice the role play in your group, using different response strategies, until you arrive at the best strategy that your group can devise.

Remind students of these guidelines for role plays:

1. The role play must be something that could really happen.

2. If the role play involves any physical contact between students, the students must agree to and practice the contact to ensure physical safety.

3. The strategy used to respond to the violence must be nonviolent, must not be superhuman, and it must create or preserve safety.

Depending on the time available, have groups share the situations and responses, or have them actually act out their role plays. As a class, talk about each situation presented. If the students are really engaged in in-depth problem solving, spend the rest of the period analyzing each situation and strategizing about how to stop and prevent the violence. If time allows, you can return to the following material in the next session.

Getting Help Exercise

In your own words, introduce the following exercise:

Think of one of the kinds of violence that you checked on the handout, or the situation you thought of at the beginning of class, and visualize the situation as you experience it in your mind.

Ask the following questions, having students think of the answers as they apply to their personal experience. Or, ask the questions one by one, and have students share their thoughts with the group. Encourage students to think of details and to think realistically.

- Think of one friend you could talk with right now about what is happening to you. What would you say? When might be a good time to talk with her or him? What kind of support would you want from that person?

- If the friend you are thinking of is a young person, who is one adult you could talk with?

- Who could you talk to in the community? Do you know of a hotline, doctor, teacher, coach, religious leader, counselor, or clinic you could contact for help? How could you find out about them if you needed to?

- What else could you do to make this situation safer for you?

Dealing with People in Power

In this exercise, the class will share their ideas on how to deal with people who are using positions of power to abuse or mistreat them.

We all have relationships with people who have some authority over us, like a teacher, an older brother or sister, an older relative, or a boss. Occasionally, in these relationships, that person can use their authority to pressure us into doing something we don't want to do, or to mistreat or abuse us.

Making the Peace

When this happens, it can be very difficult to talk to someone about the situation and to ask for help.

For example, suppose you are in a situation in which you feel your boss or supervisor is using his or her authority to push you around. What might make it difficult to leave the situation or to ask for help?

Write students' ideas on the board. Their answers might include "I'm too scared to ask for help," "I don't know how to ask for help," "I don't know what I need," "It would mean stepping out of the box," "I feel like I deserve the abuse," "I feel too vulnerable," "I have a fear of rejection," "That person could hurt me," "No one would believe me." Then, ask the same question—*What might make it difficult to leave the situation or to ask for help?*—for each of the following situations:

- a student is being pressured by a teacher

- a gang member is being pressured by a gang

- a younger sibling is being pressured by an older sibling

- a teenager is being hassled by police

- a girlfriend is being pressured by a boyfriend

- a daughter or son is being abused by a parent, stepparent, or other older relative

Have each student silently choose one phrase from the list on the board that most closely fits what has personally kept her or him from asking for help.

Closure: The Safety Plan

Distribute On Your Own sheet 12. In your own words, introduce the idea of writing a safety plan for dealing with an unsafe situation.

Everyone has the right to be safe and the right to get help when they need it. We can only make the peace when each one of us feels secure and strong enough to ask for and expect the support we need to end abusive relationships.

A safety plan is a way to get out of a dangerous place or relationship, step by step. Creating a safety plan can help us to figure out what we can do, where we can get support, and what our choices are. A safety plan often involves asking for help from others.

On the My Safety Plan sheet, you will identify a situation in which you are experiencing, or are vulnerable to, violence or abuse in your life right now. The assignment is to make a safety plan—a step-by-step plan of what you can do right now, over the next day and the next week—to get unstuck, to get help, and to get out of danger.

Use the following example, or adapt it, to review the components of a safety plan.

My Safety Plan

1. The Problem   Identify a situation in your life right now in which you feel unsafe or vulnerable to violence or abuse of any kind—at school, work, in your neighborhood, or in relationships with parents or friends.

a.   Name the problem.

My boyfriend gets very mad, hits me

b.   Name or identify the person(s) who makes you unsafe.

James

c.   Describe the problem in detail, or draw a picture of it.

He got jealous. Last Friday at a party he said I was flirting. He yelled at me and slapped me. It's happening more.

d.   Identify the lethal or most dangerous elements of this situation:

name-calling ✓	being physically restrained or trapped
yelling	unsafe activities
✓ threats	physical punishment
✓ hitting	unsafe drug use
weapons	other_____

e.   What makes it hard for you to get out of or change this situation?

I'm embarrassed, and I'm scared

f.   What makes it hard for you to ask for help to deal with this situation?

I'm embarrassed, feel stupid

g.   What will happen if you don't change the situation?

Best scenario: *It'll go on like this*

Worst scenario: *He'll really hurt me bad*

2. The Support

a.   Who do you know personally as a friend or relative who could help you to deal with this problem?

Person 1: *Sheila (friend)*

Person 2: *I don't know anybody else I could trust*

b. What are specific things they could do to help you?

Person 1   Person 2

1. *listen*

2. *give advice*

3. *talk to his friends*

4. *walk with me after school*

c. Who could you go to outside of friends or relatives?

teacher	✓ counselor	community agency
coach	✓ minister/rabbi	clinic
nurse	doctor	✓ hotline
✓ police	other	

3. The Plan

a. Identify the overall goal of your plan. *Get out of relationship*

b. Identify five major actions you can take to achieve this goal

1. *tell him*

2. *get my friend to go with me*

3. *get some advice from a hotline about protection*

4. *talk to the counselor to figure out how to keep him away*

5. *learn how to defend myself—take a class*

4. The Timeline

a. In 24 hours I will — *tell my girlfriend*

b. In 48 hours I will — *plan how to tell him and talk to hotline*

c. In one week I will — *talk to a counselor, then tell him with my girlfriend*

d. In two weeks I will — *be out of the relationship; see a counselor; find out about a self-defense class*

e. In one month I will — *start self-defense class; keep away from him*

f. In three months I will — *finish self-defense class; stay out of all relationships*

g. In six months I will — *think about whether I want to be in another relationship*

What if . . .

Students have no experience of violence? Some students will not have, or will claim not to have, any current experience of violence in their lives. Encourage them to think of any person or situation that makes them feel unsafe, scared, or threatened. If nothing comes to mind, have them think of a situation that has been related to them by a peer and try to imagine themselves in that person's place. The intention of this session is for students to have opportunities to practice thinking through what it would take to construct a safety plan and to take the necessary steps to make an unsafe situation safe.

Students have no information about resources? If students have no ideas about what resources are available in the community, you can either provide them with some phone numbers or suggest that they put together a list of resources as a project. This list could be distributed throughout the school, printed in the student newspaper, or posted in the halls or the restrooms. It could be translated into whatever languages are spoken by students and their families. If some community services are not accessible to youth, this could be an issue around which to organize student support. In some areas, adults and youth have organized teen-help hotlines or resource lines.

Check any of the following kinds of immediate or institutional violence students at your school experience, even if you think it happens to only a few students.

- ☐ male/male fights
- ☐ female/female fights
- ☐ guns on campus
- ☐ drug use
- ☐ sexual assault or rape
- ☐ family violence
- ☐ gang violence
- ☐ drive-by shootings
- ☐ segregated neighborhoods
- ☐ suicide
- ☐ eating disorders
- ☐ cutbacks in park, recreation area, or library hours
- ☐ sexual harassment or discrimination
- ☐ racial harassment or discrimination
- ☐ police harassment
- ☐ high-risk sexual behavior
- ☐ lack of decent jobs for young people
- ☐ street and neighborhood violence
- ☐ poverty in the community
- ☐ verbal abuse and harassment
- ☐ attacks against immigrants
- ☐ toxic pollution from a nearby factory
- ☐ "hate" violence
- ☐ graffiti with gender or racial slurs

Pick one type of violence you are directly involved with in some way, even if only as an observer. Write it down here.

What are the causes of this type of violence?

What can the people involved do to change?

What can people around them do to stop the violence?

What could a group of you and your friends do?

1. The Problem

Identify a situation in your life right now in which you feel unsafe or vulnerable to violence or abuse of any kind—at school, work, in your neighborhood, or in relationships with parents or friends.

a. Name the problem.

b. Name or identify the person(s) who makes you unsafe.

c. Describe the problem in detail, or draw a picture of it.

d. Identify the lethal or most dangerous elements of this situation.

name-calling	yelling	being physically restrained or trapped
unsafe activities	threats	physical punishment
hitting	unsafe drug use	weapons
other:		

e. What makes it hard for you to get out of or change this situation?

f. What makes it hard for you to ask for help to deal with this situation?

g. What will happen if you don't change the situation?

   Best scenario:

   Worst scenario:

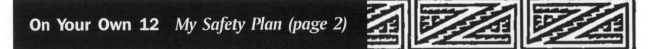

2. The Support

a. Who do you know personally as a friend or relative who could help you to deal with this problem?

Person 1:

Person 2:

Person 3:

b. What are specific things they could do to help you?

Person 1:

1.

2.

3.

4.

Person 2:

1.

2.

3.

4.

Person 3:

1.

2.

3.

4.

c. Who could you go to outside of friends or relatives?

teacher	clinic	counselor	community agency
coach	doctor	minister/rabbi	hotline
nurse	police	other:	

3. The Plan

a. Identify the overall goal of your plan.

b. Identify five major actions you can take to achieve this goal.

1.

2.

3.

4.

5.

4. The Timeline

a. In 24 hours I will:

b. In 48 hours I will:

c. In one week I will:

d. In two weeks I will:

e. In one month I will:

f. In three months I will:

g. In six months I will:

Becoming Allies

Aims

■ To strengthen every student's commitment to being an ally

■ To develop strategies to intervene in current incidents or patterns of violence affecting school and family life

■ To help students build alliances across lines of race, gender, and age

Skills

Students will

■ Understand how to be effective allies

■ Overcome fears of getting involved

■ Develop strategies for dealing with violent situations

■ Commit to being an ally

Preparation

■ You will need copies of On Your Own sheet 13. You will also need the Power Chart, and butcher paper and markers or a chalkboard and chalk.

To Begin: Overview on Becoming Allies

Take a few moments for students to discuss any thoughts, feelings, memories, or fears that were brought up by the previous session's homework, which involved looking at current experiences of violence and developing a safety plan for coping with them.

We have been looking at the violence that some of us are dealing with now, and the violence that all of us see at school, in our neighborhoods, and in our homes. Today, we will take the next step: becoming allies to each other to stop the violence.

Display the Power Chart, and review the definition of *ally* that was presented in Session 4:

An ally is a peacemaker—someone who helps break the cycle of violence. We can be allies to ourselves, to our peers, and to others across the lines of the Power Chart.

*An ally is someone who sees a fight happening, or someone being taunted with racial labels, or someone being sexually harassed, or someone hurting themselves with drugs or thinking about suicide, **and does something about it**. To make the peace in our community, we need everyone to be an ally, to take a stand against violence in any of these forms.*

As a class, develop a list of the qualities of an ally. Prompt students with the following questions:

- Using the issue for which you developed your safety plan, think about what kind of help you would want from a friend. If someone were going to come through for you, what kind of response would you need?

- What kind of attitude would you like that person to have?

- What kind of support would you need?

- What words describe what you want from an ally?

The Job of an Ally

Summarize the list students have generated into the following five qualities of an ally:

1. An ally listens.

Pay attention to, believe in, and respect what the person who needs help says.

2. An ally is present.

Back the person up—by being a friend, by keeping your word, and by letting the person know when you *can't* be there.

3. An ally opens doors.

Help the person explore the available options, resources, and support. Provide useful information, and share your resources and connections.

4. An ally takes chances.

Sometimes we don't reach out because we fear we will make a mistake or say the wrong thing. An ally is bold. When they mess up, they fix it and try again. It's always important to take a chance and reach out.

5. An ally gets support.

When you are helping someone, remember to take care of yourself. Don't do it all alone.

Next, ask students what would *not* be helpful from an ally. Make a new list of their ideas, which may include guilt, judging, giving unwanted advice, condescension, blaming, and rescuing.

Finish this discussion by having the group think about how they could apply their ideas to a real situation.

Think about a person who you know or you think needs help. Perhaps it's someone who is being abused or harassed by a parent, teacher, boyfriend, or other students; perhaps it's someone who is acting self-destructively, getting into lots of fights, or being abusive to others.

When students are ready, ask them to think about these questions:

■ How could you be an ally to that person?

■ How could you back that person up, but act honestly and honorably?

■ What could you say if your friend gets defensive? How could you respond if he or she tells you to go away?

■ Finally, what is it that gets in your way sometimes when you want to be an ally and get involved?

Ally Role Plays

Break students into groups of four or five to create ally role plays. Each group should decide on one or two situations in which someone, or a group of people, might need an ally, and then develop a role play about how someone could intervene as a powerful ally for that person or group. If there is time, each group can devise two different endings for their role play: the worst possible thing to do, and the best possible thing to do.

Depending on the time available, have one or more groups describe or act out their role plays (with both endings, if they created two endings) and talk about why the intervention they proposed would be effective. Have other students contribute ideas on what else might work in that situation. Keep the focus on realistic solutions, especially those that do not replicate or continue the violence.

It is important to acknowledge that these can be dangerous situations and that intervention should always be done cautiously and with as much support as possible. Encourage students to evaluate the level of danger in each role play so that they can learn how to make realistic choices. Sometimes the safest thing to do is to get help from someone with more power or authority, such as a teacher, administrator, or police officer.

Point out that every situation will call for a unique response and that individuals will often have to decide on the spot what is the best course of action. It helps to role play, to anticipate potential scenarios, and to share ideas so that when a situation arises that requires intervention you have lots of ideas about things to try. The goal of this exercise is not to devise "perfect" solutions but to practice problem solving and to share ideas. Students' criticisms, doubts, and reality testing should be dealt with in a spirit of sharpening everyone's ability to find realistic solutions, not to sabotage the process itself or other students' enthusiasm for becoming involved.

You may want to ask students what happens when we don't do anything because of our fear. Who gets hurt then? What are the costs?

Closure

To close the session, remind the group of the basic reasons why allies are needed.

Everyone needs powerful allies. And we can each be a powerful ally to the people around us—not only for friends or family, but for anyone in our community who is experiencing violence, injustice, or abuse.

Distribute On Your Own sheet 13, and remind the class that this is the Ally Pledge they discussed in Session 4. Ask students to review the Ally Pledge and to think seriously about whether they are ready to sign it. If so, they should sign and keep the pledge to remind themselves of their commitment to make the peace. Encourage them to talk among themselves about how to support their being able to keep their commitment to the Ally Pledge.

If this is part of a schoolwide campaign, a more public gesture of commitment may be appropriate, such as large sign-on posters. If you are using our schoolwide companion program, Days of Respect, signing the Ally Pledge might be part of that.

What if . . .

Students feel hopeless, cynical, or pessimistic about realistic solutions to violence—or pessimistic that an ally would ever back them up? Students may relate stories along the lines of, "I know someone who did that and they ended up being blown away," or have an endless series of "but what if" questions. Consider the source of such comments carefully. Students may be testing the suggestions to see whether they really believe they could work. They may have given up themselves and have no hope that *anything* will make a difference. Or, they may be scared and are simply acknowledging the level of danger that exists in their community.

Encourage other students to engage them in discussion rather than putting yourself in the position of trying to convince them that having allies can make a significant difference.

The Five Qualities of an Ally

1. An ally listens.

Pay attention to, believe in, and respect what the person who needs help says.

2. An ally is present.

Back the person up—by being a friend, by keeping your word, and by letting the person know when you *can't* be there.

3. An ally opens doors.

Help the person explore the available options, resources, and support. Provide useful information, and share your resources and connections.

4. An ally takes chances.

Sometimes we don't reach out because we fear we will make a mistake or say the wrong thing. An ally is bold. When they mess up, they fix it and try again. It's always important to take a chance and reach out.

5. An ally gets support.

When you are helping someone, remember to take care of yourself. Don't do it all alone.

Above all, an ally is a peacemaker.

> **THE ALLY PLEDGE**
>
> I pledge not to be violent to myself, my friends, my family, my lover, or anyone else. I will stand up for other people and make the peace.
>
> Signed,
>
> _____

What's Next?

Aims

- To help students to make plans for intervening in and preventing violence at school, in the community, and at home

- To have each student make a specific commitment on next steps to make the peace

- To help students appreciate one another

Skills

Students will

- Maintain a commitment to building a more peaceful environment through ongoing alliance, intervention, and action

- Understand the importance of their own actions in eliminating violence

- Continue using the Agreements, and practice using appreciation, support, and cooperation to sustain their commitments

- Begin an ongoing Making the Peace project at the school

Preparation

- You will need copies of Handouts 20, 21, and 22. You will also need butcher paper, tape, and markers.

To Begin: Overview on Reviewing the Program

Take a few moments to acknowledge that this is the last session of the Making the Peace program. Then convey the following in your own words:

This is really only the beginning of making the peace. Today we will talk about how to continue the process, for each one of us and for all of us—what we can do together, where it gets rough, and what we can do about that. So where do we go from here?
First, let's think about where we have been.

Take a minute to review the course from the beginning to prepare students for the next exercise. Two alternative ways to do this are as follows:

- As a visualization exercise: have students sit comfortably, with their eyes closed. When students are ready, take a minute or two to simply narrate the course highlights or events, or particular important moments, in chronological order.

- Less formally, ask students to take a few moments of silence to think about all that happened during the course, and then let them call out their thoughts.

Review of the Program

Put up three sheets of butcher paper with the headings "New," "Hard and Challenging," and "Roadblocks." "New" refers to ideas and understandings students have gained from the curriculum and their group discussions. "Challenging" refers to ideas that have been difficult to accept or have challenged students' thinking. "Roadblocks" refers to negative comments or thoughts or actions that came up during the process of the course, either from participants or from people students encountered outside of the program, such as friends, family members, and other teachers.

Have the students go to the lists and write their own words or phrases under any of these headings. You could begin by offering one "new" idea and one "roadblock" you experienced when you brought this program to your school or class. Make sure everyone writes at least one word or phrase on the lists.

Emphasize that, in the "Roadblocks" list, no one in the room should be blamed for something they said or did. You might frame this idea by asking students not to attach personal names to the roadblock statements or acts they remember. Also, some students may see a "roadblock" as a "challenge," or the reverse. For example, young men might say young women's anger was a roadblock rather than a challenge to men to be better allies, thereby minimizing what the young women have said. Do your best, and enlist their help, in keeping these categories separate.

NEW	HARD AND CHALLENGING	ROADBLOCKS
Being an ally	No such thing as reverse racism	Put downs
Violence happening to women	Keeping the "I-statement" agreement	Adultism from a teacher
How other students feel about violence	How to handle a fight	Attitudes of school security

When the group is through adding to the lists, let them discuss what they notice, particularly the variety of (sometimes contradictory) responses.

Next, begin another list entitled "Tools." Have students call out anything they experienced during the course that can be a *tool* for making the peace. Encourage them to think broadly about *anything* they can remember that moved the class along or helped them personally. The list might include role plays, particular agreements or the Agreements in general, working together, and particular class exercises.

Title a final list "Hot Issues" and have students generate quickly, in one- or two-word phrases, the hottest issues about violence at school, in the community, and at home—things they want to do something about. If there is time, have them review this list and suggest tools— those already listed or new ones—to deal with each issue.

Action Plans

Distribute and review Handout 20. Divide the class into small groups, and ask each group to choose a "Hot Issue" from the class list and to use the allotted time to generate a doable school activity that they or the whole class could initiate and carry through. Ask groups to follow the format on the handout as much as possible.

Have each group briefly present its plan. After each presentation, allow the entire group to offer suggestions and other resources for making it happen. Encourage anyone particularly interested in another group's plan to sign on to participate.

The Ally Pledge

Divide the class into pairs, and give each student one minute to tell their partner whether they signed the Ally Pledge, and why or why not. If they didn't sign it, ask them to talk about what support they would need to be able to sign it.

Evaluation and Ongoing Activities

(This can be done as a homework assignment if time is short, although you will get fewer responses.)

Distribute Handouts 21 and 22. Emphasize that students' evaluation of the Making the Peace program is important to you and to the class; it helps us all go on learning together what works to make the peace and what needs to be different. Have them complete and hand in the follow-up activities interest list and the evaluation (without putting their names on them). It is important that students' confidentiality is maintained for this process. You can also post the interest list and have students signal their interest in particular activities.

Closing Circle

Have the class stand in a circle. Ask each student to think about one highlight from the program, and one note of appreciation for something that another student said or did during the sessions. If there is enough time, give everyone a chance to share a highlight and an appreciation. If time is short, have a few people share their thoughts.

At the end of the circle, thank everyone for being involved and participating in the process. If appropriate, offer your continued support and resources to them to continue the project.

Dear Teacher:

We hope this curriculum has been clear, accessible, useful, and effective. We would like to have you and your students' comments, thoughts, and suggestions so that we can improve future editions and continue to strengthen our work.

We also love to hear success stories from students and teachers that we can share with students in other parts of the country. Please write us

c/o The Oakland Men's Project
1203 Preservation Park Way,
Oakland, California, 94612
or call at (510) 835-2433.

Keep on making the peace.

—Paul Kivel and Allen Creighton

1. The "Hot Issue" we have chosen is:

2. We chose this issue because:

3. This issue affects:

4. This is what we want to achieve:

5. This is what has to happen for us to achieve our goal:

6. These are possible strategies or actions we could take to achieve our goal:

   a.

   b.

   c.

   d.

7. This is the strategy we have chosen:

8. These are people we know are available to help us:

9. These are material resources we know are available to us:

10. This is the first step we need to take:

11. These are the next steps we need to take:

12. These are the final steps we need to take:

13. These are possible roadblocks to our plan:

14. These are ways to overcome these roadblocks:

15. This is how we will know our plan has worked:

There are many ways for you to continue helping to make the peace in our school. Please take a few minutes to look at the ideas below and to indicate which programs you might have an interest in being a part of. You will not put your name on this sheet, but, if there is enough interest in a particular kind of group, the school will try to establish that group on campus.

Continuing Study and Discussion

Any number of topics can be chosen for follow-up study and discussion. Groups can meet at lunch, or before or after school, and with or without adult help or leadership.

Topics I would be interested in continuing to study and discuss:

Support Groups

A support group is a group that meets to give its members support around a particular issue or concern in their lives. Support groups might have a facilitator or leader, and they can be short-term or ongoing.

Support groups I would be interested in joining:

❏ violence-free relationships

❏ sexual abuse survivors

❏ youth with jobs

❏ staying drug-free

❏ eating and weight problems

❏ other: _____

Advocacy Groups

An advocacy group consists of people who come together around an identity that they share—such as a shared ethnicity, gender, sexual orientation, religion, or economic class. The group provides support and allies for dealing with external situations.

Advocacy groups I would be interested in joining:

❏ African-American students

❏ Arab-American students

❏ Asian-American students

❑ Latino students

❑ Lesbian, gay, or bisexual students

❑ Native American students

❑ Students of color

❑ Jewish students

❑ young women

❑ young men

❑ students with disabilities

❑ other: _____

Peer Education

Peer educators are students who want to teach this curriculum or to do other violence-prevention work with students your age or younger.

❑ I would be interested in doing peer education.

Conflict Resolution and Mediation

A conflict-resolution or mediation program is one way to create peaceful alternatives to violence on campus. In this program, students who have conflicts can talk about them with peer mediators for help in solving problems.

❑ I would be interested in being involved in a conflict-resolution program.

Campus Action

A campus action group chooses a particular problem or concern and plans how to organize others—students and adults—to address that issue.

I would be interested in forming a campus action group on the following issues:

❑ violence on campus

❑ sexual harassment

❑ racism

❑ student health

❑ drug prevention

❏ neighborhood violence

❏ after-school recreation

❏ curriculum development

❏ other: _____

Days of Respect Program

Days of Respect is a schoolwide violence prevention program in which students, parents, and teachers work together to plan and implement violence prevention activities.

❏ I would be interested in having a Days of Respect program at this school.

Community Action

A community action group is like a campus action group but with a wider focus. A community action group identifies an issue and organizes people to become involved and address that issue, either by working with an existing community group or by forming a new group. There may already be many local community groups organizing around issues of safety, jobs and economic development, health, and education.

I would be interested in forming or joining a community action group on the following issues:

❏ toxics in the environment

❏ police/youth relations

❏ access to health care

❏ school district policy (curriculum development, campus safety, community control issues)

❏ job training and economic development

❏ violence against women

❏ youth recreation

❏ other: _____

Please fill out this evaluation form. You don't need to put your name on it. Your teacher can use your comments to fill in gaps in this program and to adapt it for future use.

1. Rate each of the following topics.

	Excellent		Good		Poor
a. coverage of violence	1	2	3	4	5
b. interest of material	1	2	3	4	5
c. handouts	1	2	3	4	5
d. homework	1	2	3	4	5
e. teacher presentation	1	2	3	4	5
f. clearness of ideas presented	1	2	3	4	5
g. usefulness of material	1	2	3	4	5
h. relevance of material	1	2	3	4	5

2. Did this program change your understanding of violence? If so, how?

3. Did this program change your way of taking care of yourself and getting support? If so, how?

4. Describe one situation or relationship you will deal with differently because of what you have learned in this program.

5. Did this program change the way you see other people? If so, how?

6. Have you talked about this program with anyone outside of class? If so, what is their relationship to you?

7. Are you interested in being involved in some kind of follow-up activity to this program? If so, what kind?

8. What parts of this curriculum need improvement?

   ☐ material in sessions on the following topics:

   ☐ teacher preparation   ☐ handouts   ☐ homework

9. What was left out of the program that should have been discussed?

10. What was covered too briefly?

11. What do you think are the most important aspects of being an ally?

12. Did this program help you to be a better ally to others? If so, how?

13. Please use the other side of this sheet for other comments you have about the program.

   Thank you!
We hope that you will mail these forms to us at the Oakland Men's Project so that we can improve future editions of this curriculum. You can also write to the Oakland Men's Project directly at 1203 Preservation Park Way, Oakland, CA 94612 or call us at (510) 835–2433.

Keep on making the peace!

Resources

Voices of Young People

City Kids. *City Kids Speak.* New York: Random House, 1994.

Hoose, Phillip. *It's Our World Too! Stories of Young People Making a Difference.* Boston: Little, Brown, 1993.

Kuklin, Susan. *Speaking Out: Teenagers Take on Race, Sex, and Identity.* New York: Putnam, 1993.

Schoem, David, ed. *Inside Separate Worlds: Life Stories of Young Blacks, Jews and Latinos.* Ann Arbor, MI: Prentice-Hall, 1991.

Singer, Bennett L., ed. *Growing Up Gay: A Literary Anthology.* New York: New Press, 1993.

Working with Young People

Cohen, Richard. *Students Resolving Conflict: Peer Mediation in Schools.* New York: Good Year Books/HarperCollins, 1995.

Creighton, Allan, with Paul Kivel. *Helping Teens Stop Violence: A Practical Guide for Counselors, Educators, and Parents.* Alameda, CA: Hunter House, 1992.

——— *Young Men's Work: Building Skills to Stop Violence.* Center City, MN: Hazelden, 1995.

Goldstein, Arnold P., et al. *Aggression Replacement Training: A Comprehensive Intervention for Aggressive Youth.* Champaign, IL: Research Press, 1987.

Heath, Shirley Brice, and Milbrey W. McLaughlin, eds. *Identity and Inner-City Youth: Beyond Ethnicity and Gender.* New York: Teachers College Press, 1993.

Hipp, Earl. *The Caring Circle: A Facilitator's Guide to Support Groups.* Center City, MN: Hazelden, 1992.

Johnson, Kendall, Ph.D. *School Crisis Management: A Hands-On Guide to Training Crisis Response Teams.* Alameda, CA: Hunter House, 1993.

Miedzian, Myriam. *Boys Will Be Boys: Breaking the Link Between Masculinity and Violence.* New York: Doubleday, 1991.

Rochman, Hazel. *Against Borders: Promoting Books for a Multicultural World.* Chicago: American Library Association/Booklist Publications, 1993.

Teaching Tolerance magazine. 400 Washington Ave., Montgomery, AL 36104.

Vasquez, Hugh, and Isoke Femi. *No Boundaries: A Manual for Unlearning Oppression and Building Multicultural Alliances.* TODOS Institute, 1203 Preservation Park Way, Oakland, CA 94612; 1993.

Wittmer, Joe, and Robert D. Myrick. *The Teacher as Facilitator.* Minneapolis, MN: Educational Media, 1989.

On the Issues

Children's Safety Network. *Firearm Facts.* Arlington, VA: National Center for Education in Maternal and Child Health, 1994.

Kivel, Paul. *Men's Work: How to Stop the Violence That Tears Our Lives Apart.* Center City, MN: Hazelden, 1992.

———— *Uprooting Racism: How White People Can Work for Racial Justice.* Gabriola Island, B.C. & Philadelphia, PA: New Society Publishers, 1995.

Levy, Barrie. *Dating Violence: Young Women in Danger.* Seattle, WA: Seal Press, 1991.

Males, Mike A. *The Scapegoat Generation: America's War on Adolescents.* Monroe, ME: Common Courage Press, 1996.

Rethinking Schools Collective. *Rethinking Our Classrooms: Teaching for Equity and Justice.* Milwaukee, WI: Rethinking Schools, 1994.

Sklar, Holly. *Chaos or Community: Seeking Solutions, Not Scapegoats for Bad Economics.* Boston: South End Press, 1995.

Stoltenberg, John. *The End of Manhood: A Book for Men of Conscience.* New York: Dutton, 1993.

Tavris, Carol. *Anger: The Misunderstood Emotion.* New York: Simon and Schuster, 1982.

Activities for Young People

Bass, Ellen, and Kate Kaufman. *Free Your Mind: The Book for Gay, Lesbian, and Bisexual Youth—and Their Allies.* New York: Harper Collins, 1996.

Brody, Ed, et al. *Spinning Tales, Weaving Hope: Stories of Peace, Justice and the Environment.* Philadelphia, PA & Gabriola Island, B.C.: New Society Publishers, 1992.

Creighton, Allan, and Paul Kivel. *Young Men's Work: Building Skills to Stop Violence.* Center City, MN, Hazelden 1995.

Donahue, David M., and Nancy Flowers. *The Uprooted: Refugees and the United States.* Alameda, CA: Hunter House, 1995.

Duvall, Lynn. *Respecting Our Differences: A Guide to Getting Along in a Changing World.* Minneapolis, MN: Free Spirit Publishing, 1994.

Fleisher, Paul. *Changing Our World: A Handbook for Young Activists.* Tucson, AZ: Zephyr Press, 1993.

Fleugelman, Andrew, ed. *The New Games Book.* Garden City, NJ: Doubleday, 1976.

———— *More New Games and Playful Ideas.* Garden City, NJ: Doubleday, 1981.

Hazouri, Sandra Peyser, and Miriam Smith McLaughlin. *Warm Ups and Wind Downs: 101 Activities for Moving and Motivating Groups.* Minneapolis, MN: Educational Media, 1993.

Healthy Relationships: A Violence-Prevention Curriculum. Men for Change, Box 33005, Quinpool Postal Outlet, Halifax, Nova Scotia, Canada B3L 4T6; 1992.

Hipp, Earl. *Feed Your Head: Some Excellent Stuff on Being Yourself.* Center City, MN: Hazelden, 1991.

Johnson, Kendall, Ph.D. *Turning Yourself Around: Self-Help for Troubled Teens.* Alameda, CA: Hunter House, 1992.

Kreidler, William J. *Conflict Resolution in the Middle School: A Curriculum and Teaching Guide.* Cambridge, MA: Educators for Social Responsibility, 1994.

Levy, Barrie. *In Love and in Danger: A Teen's Guide to Breaking Free of Abusive Relationships.* Seattle, WA: Seal Press, 1993.

Lewis, Barbara A. *The Kid's Guide to Social Action: How to Solve the Social Problems You Choose—and Turn Creative Thinking into Positive Action.* Minneapolis, MN: Free Spirit Press, 1991

Muse, Daphne, ed. *Prejudice: Stories About Hate, Ignorance, Revelation, and Transformation.* New York: Hyperion Books, 1995.

Orlick, Terry. *The Cooperative Sports and Games Book: Challenge Without Competition.* New York: Pantheon Books, 1978.

——— *The Second Cooperative Sports and Games Book.* New York: Pantheon Books, 1982.

Rose, Stephen J. *Social Stratification in the United State: The American Profile Poster.* New York: New Press, 1992.

Schniedewind, Nancy, and Ellen Davidson. *Open Minds to Equality: A Sourcebook of Learning Activities to Promote Race, Sex, Class and Age Equity.* Englewood Cliffs, NJ: Prentice-Hall, 1983.

Strauss, Susan, with Pamela Espeland. *Sexual Harassment and Teens: A Program for Positive Change.* Minneapolis, MN: Free Spirit, 1992.

Notes

Notes

Notes

Notes

Making the Peace

DAYS OF RESPECT: Organizing a School-Wide Violence Prevention Program *by* Ralph Cantor with Paul Kivel, Allan Creighton, and the Oakland Men's Project — **From the the authors of** *Making the Peace*

A unique, collaborative program that empowers students to create a climate of respect and tolerance in their school

In too many American schools, each day brings the possibility of violence when students, teachers, or parents may be harassed, assaulted, or even killed. The Days of Respect program, developed by an experienced teacher and the Oakland Men's project, speaks directly to young people's immediate need for participation, and respect. It brings students, teachers, administrators, parents, and members of the community together to create a school-wide event on the theme of violence prevention. The **Days of Respect** program:

- Enlists and prepares students to become leaders in creating a school-wide climate of respect and mobilizes every student to decrease violence

- Develops active family and community participation with students in building respect

- Engages and mobilizes every student to decrease violence

- Establishes a permanent, collaborative, democratic problem-solving and violence-reduction process within the school

With this hands-on organizer's manual, all the tools and information needed to run an exciting and inspiring Days of Respect program are at your fingertips. Drawing on successful presentations in several schools, the manual **includes reproducible handouts:** outlines, timelines, agendas, training exercises, a guide for media outreach, and step-by-step instructions for staging the event.

Ralph J. Cantor has been a high school teacher and counselor for over twenty-five years, and holds master's degrees in teaching and counseling.

64 pages ... 6 b&w photos ... Paperback ... $14.95

Junior High School Curriculum: In September 2000, we will publish a companion curriculum to *Making the Peace* intended for Junior High and Middle School, with several completely new activities and handouts. Please call after March 2000 for further details and price.

HELPING TEENS STOP VIOLENCE: A Practical Guide for Counselors, Educators, and Parents _by_ Allan Creighton, Battered Women's Alternatives with Paul Kivel, Oakland Men's Project

> _"We believe individual acts of violence are expressions of much broader patterns of social violence, and that social violence is an expression of long-standing power imbalances between 'have' and 'have not' groups in our society. What we see from day to day are the high percentage of individuals involved; what we rarely hear about are the broader imbalances that motivate the violence...."_ — From the book

Today's teenagers live in a violent world. They are subject to abuse at home, at school, and in social situations. For the past fourteen years, the nationally acclaimed Oakland Men's Project (OMP) and Battered Women's Alternatives (BWA) have been conducting seminars and workshops with teens and adults around the country, weaving issues of gender, race, age, and sexual orientation into frank discussions about male violence and its roots.

This new book by the founders of OMP and BWA provides guidelines on how to help teenagers help themselves out of the cycle of abuse. Their program provides the groundwork for working with teens to reduce the violence in their lives and in the world around them. Topics include:

- How to initiate discussions with teens about violence and uncover its root causes
- How role plays can aid in exploring issues of race, gender, and sexual orientation
- How to help teens set up peer support groups
- What steps to follow when helping abused teens

> _"Beyond the role play, the support group, and the trained volunteers, this educational process pictures adults and young people finding a common cause, common language, and a common understanding to face the very real conditions that limit us all."_ — Family Violence & Sexual Assault Bulletin

168 pages ... 16 b&w photos ... Paperback $14.95 ... Spiral bound $17.95

Interested in a _Making the Peace_ training?

For more information about the trainings and programs offered by the Oakland Men's Project, please contact them at:

OMP/TODOS
MAKING THE PEACE Program
1203 Preservation Park Way, Suite 200
Oakland, CA 94612
Phone 510-444-6448 • Fax 510-835-2466 • E-mail todos@igc.apc.org

All prices subject to change

SCHOOL CRISIS MANAGEMENT: A Team Training Guide *by* Kendall Johnson, Ph.D.

This detailed guide will prepare schools to handles crises, from large emergencies such as earthquakes and floods, to local and urgent problems such as suicide, terrorism, and gang violence. Full-page charts accompany each area of discussion throughout the book. These can be reproduced as overhead transparencies or copied for staff training sessions. Strategies are included for staff burnout, team selection, and community involvement. **Includes 78 reproducible handouts and overheads.**

192 pages ... 78 charts and diagrams ... Paperback $19.95 ... Spiral $24.95

TRAUMA IN THE LIVES OF CHILDREN: Crisis and Stress Management Techniques for Counselors, EMTs, and Other Professionals *by* Kendall Johnson, Ph.D. ... New second edition

Written by one of the foremost trauma experts in the country, this book explains how schools, therapists, and families can and must work together to help children traumatized by natural disasters, parental separation, violence, suicide, death of a loved one, or any other trauma a child may face.

> *"Dr. Johnson, master teacher and therapist, is to be congratulated on an important contribution. This book deserves to be read by every professional who cares for children."*
>
> — Spencer Eth, M.D., Chief of Psychiatry, V.A. Medical Center

352 pages ... Paperback $19.95 ... 2nd Edition

THE UPROOTED: REFUGEES AND THE U.S.— A Multidisciplinary Teaching Guide *by* Dave Donahue and Nancy Flowers with Amnesty International

As the global community shrinks, the U.S. community grows more diverse. Sensitivity to cultural differences is crucial in the education of our children. This book provides curricular material that encourages awareness of refugee experiences throughout history and today, in our own communities. Appendices include a bibliography, filmography, list of refugee organizations, and the Declaration of Human Rights.

All the activities can be used independently and are accompanied by ready-to-use handouts and suggestions for further study and action. A teaching bibliography, filmography, and complete list of refugee resources are included. Includes reproducible handouts. As reviewed in Teaching Tolerance.

224 pages ... 34 illus. ... Paperback $19.95 ... Spiral $24.95

ORDER FORM

NAME

ADDRESS

CITY/STATE   ZIP/POSTCODE

PHONE   COUNTRY (outside of U.S.)

TITLE	QTY		PRICE	TOTAL
Making the Peace (paperback)		@	$ 24.95	
Days of Respect (paperback)		@	$ 14.95	
Special Offer MTP899a (2 FREE Posters*)		@	$ 39.90	
Special Offer MTP899b (4 FREE Posters*)		@	$ 54.85	

*See page 1 for special offers. Prices subject to change without notice

Please list other titles below:

		@	$
		@	$
		@	$
		@	$
		@	$

Check here to receive our book catalog ☐ FREE

Shipping Costs:
First book: $3.00 by book post ($4.50 by UPS, Priority Mail, or to ship outside the U.S.) Each additional book: $1.00
For rush orders and bulk shipments call us at (800) 266-5592

TOTAL
Less discount @____%   (_____)
TOTAL COST OF BOOKS   _____
Calif. residents add sales tax   _____
Shipping & handling   _____
TOTAL ENCLOSED   _____

Please pay in U.S. funds only

☐ Check ☐ Money Order ☐ Visa ☐ Mastercard ☐ Discover

Card # _____ Exp. date_____

Signature _____

Complete and mail to:
Hunter House Inc., Publishers
PO Box 2914, Alameda CA 94501-0914
Orders: (800) 266-5592   email: ordering@hunterhouse.com
Phone (510) 865-5282 Fax (510) 865-4295
☐ Check here to receive our book catalog

MTH-R3 11/99